# THE FATHER, THE SON, AND THE AHA MOMENT

## TOOLS FOR HELPING YOU AND YOUR CHILD DEVELOP A PATH TO HAPPINESS

### STEVE AND SPENCER BARTON

# ADVANCE PRAISE

"In this very thought-provoking book, Stephen and Spencer Barton outline how to use a mindset approach to get outcomes that are intentional and real. The approach is simple and powerful but takes time to perfect. In *The Father, the Son, and the Aha Moment*, they discuss how to use this approach in parenting, but it can be used in any daily situation. Enjoy the read."

— MARY ANNE WALK, RETIRED EXECUTIVE

"*The Father, the Son, and the Aha Moment* provides solid tools for not only being a better parent, but for also navigating one's whole life. All with just a subtle shift of perspective and focus."

— TOM HOPKINS, INDUSTRIAL AUTOMATION<br>SPECIALIST, AND FATHER OF TWO BEAUTIFUL<br>ADULT DAUGHTERS

"If you are a parent and are looking for some great practices to improve your relationships and connect more deeply with your child or children, Stephen and Spencer Barton have created a fascinating practice that will help you and your children bond deeper and have more connection and fun. *The Father, the Son, and the Aha Moment* is a wealth of wisdom!"

"'You are your thoughts' gets expanded by Stephen Barton's Game of Ten. This author's game takes the reader into a new, healthier territory of self-reflection and self-renewal."

"*The Father, the Son, and the Aha Moment* is a great introduction to raising your awareness to a level Ten. It helps with overcoming the key obstacles faced with creating positive changes in everyday life and not feeling bad for doing so."

"Stephen and Spencer Barton have written a book that is nicely organized and clearly explained. It was easy to read, with great examples. I love the personal stories!"

"One thing I liked about *The Father, the Son, and the Aha Moment* is how relatable it was to my own situation being a parent and desiring a better bond with my adult child. This book comes with great tools and examples to explain how you can achieve the aha in your own life."

"I loved *The Father, the Son, and the Aha Moment*. Great content and exceptionally important in these times. The authors make it seem so simple, but we all know it's hard to change our mindsets after years of our experiences, lessons learned, and societal conditioning. My new watch words are 'take Ten!'"

# CONTENTS

*To Enoch Barton (April 20, 1932)*
*and Mary Barton (August 1, 1931 – November 24, 2021).*
*To all the parents who are doing the best they can with the awareness*
*they have.*

# FOREWORD

I was thrilled to read *The Father, the Son, and the Aha Moment* by father and son coauthors Steve and Spencer Barton. *The Father, the Son, and the Aha Moment: Tools for Helping You and Your Child Develop a Path to Happiness* is not just a book for parents, but for everyone who is looking to raise their awareness and bring about positive changes in their lives. Filled with profound wisdom and deep insight, this book gives the reader a unique perspective from a loving parent-child relationship while providing practical tools to elevate your mindset using The Game of Ten.

I first met Steve through Marianne Williamson (we are both huge fans) as students of *A Course in Miracles*. We became certified together in Miracle-Minded Coaching. Steve told me about a process he had developed to raise human awareness; I was intrigued! The more I started to understand the duality of The Game Often Played (which most of us play) and The Game of Ten (higher awareness), I realized that Steve had discovered a new technique to help others raise their consciousness and feel complete.

"You have to write a book!" I told Steve with excitement.

"You can help so many people!" Steve proceeded to tell me how much his technique helped him and his teenage son, Spencer, through difficult times in their lives, and how they now have a wonderful, strong, father-son bond with deep mutual respect and understanding.

"You and Spencer have to write a book!" I proclaimed, and soon after, as they had been hoping to for many years, they began writing this book into reality.

With the knowledge that everyone is doing the best they can with the awareness they have, The Game of Ten provides a framework to help people remain present and peaceful within their minds. This transition from a normal way of thinking to a natural one is a much-needed paradigm shift during these trying times. I can't wait to put these concepts into action in my own life and play The Game of Ten!

Therefore, dear reader, if you are ready to level up your awareness and gain the peace of mind you desire, this book is for you. Through its multitude of interesting stories, tips, and techniques, you are sure to gain profound insight on how to live a fulfilled life. Namaste.

> — TAZEEN CHOWDHURY, MIRACLE-MINDED
> LIFE COACH AND BESTSELLING AUTHOR OF
> BROWN GIRLS RISE UP!

# DO YOU HAVE WHAT IT TAKES TO BE A GREAT PARENT?

B ecause you are reading this book, you are most likely asking yourself, "How can I be the best parent for my child?" There is no one answer. There is no one solution for everyone. Everyone is different in their own way. In a parent-child relationship, you both bring your past baggage and conditioning into present interactions.

Do you experience your life? It sounds like a silly question, but do you taste every bite of food? Do you appreciate the feeling of warm socks, of a breeze on your face? Do you enjoy the songs of birds or frogs or crickets, even if you hear them every day? Before you can have appreciation, you must have awareness. Awareness and attention are taken to mean slightly different things in this book. Attention directs and focuses awareness on some subject while often blocking out other information. Awareness is the most fundamental experience of consciousness, of unbiased, unafraid observation, perception, and knowing.

The content of this book isn't the kind of thing you were taught in school; it's not taught in many self-help books or therapy sessions either, though bits and pieces are. Often, we live our lives on autopilot, in default mode, in habitual action, or panicked reaction. It can be easy to end up parenting in this manner, taking what seems to be the path of least resistance, but which turns out to be the painful path of least awareness. Some unaware actions will end up working out for the best, but many unaware actions will lead to suffering. Perhaps you've thought that if you just knew what was best for yourself and your child, then this whole thing would be a lot easier.

Of course, the world doesn't magically tell us what is best. The fact remains, your child needs to be parented. They are looking to you, whether you are a single parent, co-parent, or part of a nuclear family. Your child is a human being you have taken responsibility to raise into adulthood and to care for even beyond. My son didn't come with an instructional handbook on how to raise him. I doubt your child came with one either. All the questions that come up can be overwhelming. When parenting after a divorce or tragedy, it can be a struggle to make it through a day without feeling fear, self-doubt, anxiety, depression, and the grief of loss and abandonment; never mind holding down a full-time job and the responsibility of maintaining a home.

If you're like most parents, you've probably realized that your child is better off with you than without you. You might rationalize the situation by telling yourself that children are resilient. Indeed, children are resilient, but also impression-able and sensitive. You want to be the best role model and provider to ensure that your child will be a happy, healthy, and kind member of society. You could be unwittingly passing on your fears and neuroses, but how would you know? Is it already too late? You may be asking, "Do I even know who my child really is? Do I even know who I am?"

In September 2015, at the age of fifty-eight, I was asked to leave the home of my dreams. My wife of nineteen years, mother of our son Spencer, later informed me that she didn't want to be married to me anymore. She explained to me that I was "too much." Looking back with objectivity and forgiveness six years later, both Spencer and I were diagnosed with inattentive ADHD (ADD) in 2020, and that aspect of my behavior alone would have been too much for some people.

I was devastated. I later discovered that her friends knew of her deep unhappiness with me long before I did. The irony is, I coach awareness. My coaching practice was gaining traction when my life as I knew it came crashing down. I lost my wife, her family, and her friends, as often happens in a divorce.

I had sold all my income-producing assets to buy our dream home on the water in Maine. We had a prenuptial agreement, and the financial future on my end did not look promising. It felt like all my dreams for a happy and secure life with my family had been taken away. It felt like a tragic death. When all was said and done, I felt I had ended up with a lot less than I came into the marriage with.

One thing I knew: my love for Spencer is real, and he will always be my son. When I first left the house, I believed I would be coming back. There was a two-month separation agreement that I later discovered was not the temporary arrangement I had been told it was. I found out at the marriage counselor's office; there was never a possibility that my wife and I were getting back together. She handed me divorce papers as soon as I walked into that office. The counselor had never seen papers served in his office before.

It was game on. I immediately called my attorney to find out about my options for parental rights with Spencer. The attorney asked me, "How often do you see your son now?"

"I pick him up from school, and we talk every day on the phone," I said.

His reply was, "That's all you're going to see him unless you demand half custody." As soon as I got off the phone, I called Spencer's mother and did just that.

For the two months before being served divorce papers, I lived with my sister and her fiancé. Spencer lived there every other week. We waited for an apartment over my parents' two-car garage to become available on December 1. There was no family discount on it, yet there was a benefit. There was a door leading to the main house and a finished basement and spare bedroom where Spencer and his dog Periwinkle (Peri), a thirty-pound white labradoodle, lived and slept when not with me.

Spencer was thirteen at the time and didn't know my eighty-five-year-old parents as intimately as he knew his mother's parents. Living with my parents every other week gave him an opportunity to know them better than he otherwise would have. We were settling into the new normal. Spencer lived with me one week on and one week off, moving in with me for a week, then moving back to his mother's house.

Ram Dass is credited with saying, "If you think you're enlightened, go spend a week with your family." This was so true. I found myself in a situation that felt unbelievable. I was living in my parents' home without a job while raising a son.

I had never had anxiety before, and then at fifty-eight, there it was. I was previously in the flower business with my father, which I ran for thirty years. We became the largest in the state, and it never caused me anxiety. My world had come crashing down, and I was living with my father, who consistently told my siblings and mother that he ran the business, and if it weren't for him, I'd be homeless. When in fact, I started running the family business at age twenty-two after he had a major stroke and was physically and emotionally unable to work there. Ken Blanchard called it "seagull management." My father was able to fly in, shit on everyone, and fly out, leaving me to clean up the mess.

I remember lying on the couch in the apartment, waiting to pick Spencer up from school. A wave of anxiety came over me like I had never felt before. I remember saying to myself, "A breath. I have a breath." I had no words, but I had my breath. I lost myself. I felt that I had lost everything else, and I didn't know if I would lose my son too. The waves would come and go. I had no prior experience with it. It felt like I was living in dread, grief, and fear. This went on for a year and a half.

Even writing this now, I realize how vulnerable I was. After dealing with this anxiety for over a year, the central concept of *A Course in Miracles* came into my mind, and I thought, "Nothing real can be threatened. Nothing unreal exists. Herein lies the peace of God." Then another, by Marianne Williamson, "Our deepest fear is not that we are inadequate. Our deepest fear is that we are powerful beyond measure."

At that moment, I realized there is only love. The anxiety I was feeling was love trying to return to my body. I had given my power away, and it was waiting for me to allow it back inside. I talked to the wave of love and asked for it to come into my body as the love that it is. It was almost instantaneous. The anxiety was there to be seen and felt for what it was, love returning.

The anxiety was gone. I knew what it was. I had given my power away to my *idea* of my situation. The love outside of myself appeared for a couple of days, and I continued to welcome it back into me with open arms. I had overcome my anxiety and have not experienced it since.

We have the ability to give our power away to our idea of a person or situation. This leads to feelings of frustration, anxiety, and depression. We also have the ability to honor our power, in a state of grace, joy, and peace, even during difficult times. I hope to give you the tools in the upcoming chapters to understand and maintain your power and to share this ability with others.

Maybe you feel like seeking advice from family members, other parents, a clergyman, or other members of your community. While there is valuable advice out there, you may hear a lot of, "It will all work out, don't overthink it," and "Everyone is just winging it, don't let them kid you." You don't buy this reassurance, and deep down, you know there's a different way, but you can't quite figure it out. It's frustrating, and the more frustrating it is, the more you react to situations from frustration. Perhaps you've become their firefighter, racing to solve problems for your child, whether at their school or at home. It's exhausting at best; you never know if you're doing a good job parenting. Even when others tell you that you are, they don't know what you're going through. Perhaps you feel that you are a fake, a phony, an imposter. You may think, "If only they knew how I feel at this moment and how poorly I would grade myself as a parent." You may feel that you have to be polite and thank them for thinking you're doing a good job, yet you walk away feeling they don't have any idea what they're talking about.

Perhaps all you require to feel reassured is to check in with your child every day and ask them, "How was your day?" If they answer, "good," then all feels well until the next day. You take a deep breath, thankful that there are no problems to deal with, because if there were, you don't feel that you have the skills or the knowledge to handle them.

So, days turn into weeks, and weeks into months, and months into years, and life goes on. You never quite know if you are doing the best for your child. You end up continually second-guessing yourself and worrying about how things will turn out. You begin telling yourself that you are not enough, you don't do enough, and you don't have enough skills to be a great parent. You may ask yourself, "What makes you think you're a great parent?"

As you well know, being a parent is, in many ways, the most important role you'll ever take on. You wish to raise your child to respect themselves and others, and to be a happy and helpful member of society. You likely want them to one day have the ability to earn money, to support themselves, and even have a family of their own. It's a responsibility not to be taken lightly or left to chance. You hope to give them the tools to be a well-rounded adult, as well as a parent or mentor to someone in the next generation. You want them to make a difference in a world that can certainly use it. To give children the confidence and knowledge to be loving, strong, wise, and accepting toward themselves and others, is the highest goal of parenthood.

It's time to stop playing small. It's time to let go of your inner child's pain, and to stop parenting from that place of pain and fear. Such parenting fills the world with more hurt children projecting this pattern onto future generations. When raising your child or children, it is your responsibility to be as mentally, physically, and emotionally healthy as possible in your situation.

Maybe this book can help you. Maybe you can find some answers here. If you get just one useful insight from our work, it will have been well worth it. Perhaps you're willing to try anything at this point. Your intuition is guiding you right now. It has guided you thus far and will always guide you to your highest good. Do you want to learn your lessons through joy or through suffering? We believe this book will answer most, if not all, of the troubling questions you have been asking yourself. You will learn that there is a way to live and parent as your authentic self, a way that you've always known, yet haven't known how to access.

In this book, you will find many concepts with which you are probably familiar, yet said in a way that you have never read or heard before. Seeing old things in new ways can lead to new awareness, and awareness is the key to everything. By the end of this book, you will have the confidence and tools to guide yourself and experience new ideas and possibilities. You will be able to test and apply the information presented and pass on this wisdom to your child, creating a loving parent-child bond which you may have never thought possible.

# 2

# LIFE CHANGES AND CHALLENGES

I worked in my family's floral business for thirty years; I was the third generation. I graduated from The University of Southern Maine in 1979 with a BS in Business Management. I went to work in the business a few months after graduation. During (and after) my first year working at the shop, I realized my father and I were like oil and water. I had always known I'd be in the business, and it was my passion, yet I knew working with my father was not an excellent choice for me.

I gave my notice, broke up with my girlfriend, and booked a one-way ticket to France, with plans to work in Holland or Germany. That was where I thought the floral and design business was *happening* in 1980. I was excited and ready. I had been to Europe twice before. In 1972, when I was sixteen, Westbrook High School sponsored a ten-day all-inclusive ski trip to Switzerland for $300 per student (I know, right?). Two years later, my brother and I toured Europe for seven weeks. That budget was $450 (about as cheap as humanly possible). You can only imagine the places we stayed and the people we met, mostly wonderful, and sometimes bizarre.

My mother and father were at an FTD floral convention in Kansas City, Missouri. Three days before I was set to leave for France, my younger sister Shirley called me. She sounded upset. She managed to get out, "Dad had a major stroke, and they're flying him home tomorrow."

My father was forty-eight at the time, a three-pack-a-day smoker, always running on nerves and caffeine. My European plans evaporated. I was managing the shop at twenty-two years old. Thank God, at least I had a business degree and a passion for floral design to draw from.

I'm pretty sure that the average age of the employees I managed was forty-five. It wasn't a smooth transition. I was met with a lot of resistance; they were not going to be managed by someone who was in diapers when they started in the business.

My father never fully recovered his functioning and had some difficulty with fine motor skills in his hands. He quit smoking and joined an exercise program run by the University of Southern Maine athletic department. He went three times a week, where he walked, jogged, and socialized. He is now eighty-nine and lives at home, where he lived happily with my ninety-year-old mother until she passed away while we were editing this book, just before Thanksgiving.

Even while recovering from the stroke, there was never a day when he didn't make it clear he was the boss. Not once, in the thirty years that I ran the company, was it easy to work with my father. I was met with resistance every step of the way. One day, I remember asking my father, "Do you want to be my father or my boss?" His reply, without hesitation, was, "I want to be your boss." My heart sank. I was still determined to grow the business and be financially secure. I also knew what I was dealing with, and working for my father was not going to be easy.

In 1985 I received a phone call from a flower shop owner in downtown Portland. The owner decided to retire due to worsening arthritis in his hands. He asked if I wanted to buy his flower shop. He told me the price, and I asked if the building was also for sale. He was renting the building and said he would ask. The building was owned by several family members in a trust. They all would have to sign off before any sale could happen.

I called my father and said, "I want to buy the Portland flower shop." He said, "No," and that he did not need any more headaches. I replied, "I'm buying it with or without you." Eventually, he agreed that buying it would be the better choice. Within a year, we purchased the building and the business for $200,000. We became the largest floral company in the state. During the twenty-nine years running the shops, we grew ten-fold. We sold the business to a local couple in November 2007, a few months before the "great recession." My father said, "How did you know?" That was one of a handful of compliments I ever received from him. I replied, "Because I'm smart."

I'm sharing this story to show that I'm familiar with the difficult dynamics of many father-son relationships. I can forgive my father because I knew that his father George, my grandfather, told him from the day he could remember, "I never wanted you to be born." George's mother had also told George that he was unwanted. George never knew his biological father. He was physically beaten and psychologically abused. He passed this abuse on to his three sons, including my father, Enoch.

I was beaten once. I was around eleven when I made a sarcastic comment to my mother in response to a question. My mother reacted by grabbing a hard-bristled hairbrush and beating and slapping my neck. My father got involved, holding me down to expose the back of my neck. I was yelling and crying for them to stop.

When they did, they realized what they had done. They apologized and hugged me. My mother told me not to tell anyone as she put concealing makeup on my neck to hide the bruises, then she drove me to Sunday school. I laugh looking back at how I was parented and how times have changed, mainly for the better, and yet, for the sake of humanity, even more awareness is needed to maintain and promote our children's physical and mental health.

I forgive them, and I love them, but I do not condone all of their past behaviors. My parents did not have the tools to parent me the way I wanted to be parented. My older brother and younger sister may have had different experiences. I suspect that many adults out there feel the same way. I understand now; they did the best they could with the parenting skills and awareness they had.

## STEVE'S CHANGE

Years later, I was in my fourteenth year running the flower shops. I was thirty-six years old. I was married to my first wife at the time. (She was the girlfriend I briefly broke up with when I was heading off to Europe.) She worked her way up from the four-midnight shift to store manager and eventually a vice president of Maine's most prominent family-owned retail company. One morning, before work, I asked her the name of the therapist that she had told me about a while back, one whom many of her colleagues went to see. The company management staff worked more than sixty hours a week. There seemed to never be enough hours in the day to get their work done. She got back to me with the therapist's name, and I made an appointment.

My first wife's best childhood friend had let me borrow three Marianne Williamson tapes and told me to get *A Course in Miracles*. I knew nothing about the contents of the book. While at the bookstore, I was also compelled to *buy Seven Habits of Highly Effective People* by Stephen Covey and Elizabeth Kubler Ross's book, *Death and Dying*.

Two weeks before my first therapy session, I had gone to a channeler/ medium/ tarot reader, Sandra J. It was my yearly treat, to dabble in the unknown world of metaphysics. This was my third year going to see her. While doing the reading, she froze abruptly. The Tower Card lay at the center of the reading. The medium locked eyes with me and said, "Look at me. You're going to go through it. It's going to be big. Make sure that you eat and make sure that you sleep." I had no idea what she was talking about.

In the meantime, I read all the books that I had bought at the bookstore. I was obsessed with what I was reading, absorbing as much as I was able. All the books essentially said the same thing, that we are all connected as one, only each said it differently. It was like I had stumbled upon the truth, and apparently, I was starving for it.

The day came for my first therapy session ever. I had no idea what to expect. I remember sitting in the waiting area, listening to the steadily purring white noise machine outside the office door. I was going to be in there soon. A person came out of the therapist's office wiping their eyes. I can't even remember if it was a man or a woman. They walked by me with no acknowledgment.

After about ten minutes, the therapist, Larry R., invited me into his office. He was an older man in his mid-seventies. I sat on the couch, and he sat in a leather swivel chair. My first insight was when he asked, "Do you have siblings? I replied, "Yes." Then he asked, "Where are you in order of age with them?" I replied, "In the middle." He said, "How does that feel?" I was always in the middle with friends and family, and it sucked. I shut that pattern down from that point on. I remember thinking, this therapy thing is going to be good.

Then Larry asked me, "Why are you here?" I replied, "I have everything in the world that I want, and I'm not happy. That's fucked up." I asked him, "What will I get from this, and how long will it take?" He responded, "Mental health, and usually I tell people three months, but you're halfway there." I guess knowing you're messed up is the halfway mark to achieving mental health.

So, I thought, "Why don't I start things off by telling him everything, from my earliest memories, until the events that brought me into his office?" It was oversharing at its finest; no holds barred. He didn't seem shocked by anything I threw out there. I'm sure he had heard a lot of figuratively and literally insane stories in his years of practice. After telling him a dozen or more things that may need to be addressed, I said, "That felt good." I visualized a pile of guilt, shame, fear, anger, sadness, abuse, and self-doubt all heaped in the middle of his office. I said, "I'm leaving this crap here." He replied, "I don't want it." We laughed together as the hour was wrapping up, and he said to me, "You know what you need to do," I wasn't quite sure what I needed to do, yet, somehow, I instinctually and intuitively found my answer.

To prepare for my next session, I knew that I needed to forgive my father. I knew I had to let go of all the secrets and shame I held inside myself. One Sunday afternoon, I drove to the family lake house, where my parents have spent every summer since 1972. I went there alone and had a quick visit before asking that I talk with my father alone. My mother and father were in the kitchen. My father did not want to speak with me. I was determined to have that talk. I repeated, "Come outside and talk with me." He replied, "No." Then for some reason, I repeated calmly, "I love you. I love you. I love you." He began yelling to my mother, "Make him stop! Make him stop!" I felt like I was in the eye of a tornado. I kept repeating, "I love you." My mother yelled for me to stop, and I continued. Amid all the yelling for me to stop, I had never felt such inner peace.

Finally, I said, "I'll stop if he comes outside and talks with me." He reluctantly agreed, and we walked outside. We sat in lawn chairs on the flagstone patio. I told my father that I knew all the family secrets, and he confirmed them. I knew that, in holding on to these secrets, I was holding on to guilt, shame, and blame. I had been blaming my father for his reprehensible actions and holding on to the pain they had caused. I told my father that I had known the secrets for a long time and that I forgave him and loved him. I felt we had the best father-son talk ever. It seemed like our talk lasted two hours; I have no idea how long it really did.

Afterward, I hugged my mother and father, told them I loved them, and left. Driving away from the lake house, I felt a lightness inside and out. I can only describe it as a cocaine high, without the cocaine. I thought to myself, "Wow! This stuff really works!" My homework was complete for my next session.

I went to the second therapy session and was happy to report about my conversation with my father. I told the therapist all the details, and I told him that I was on a natural high after forgiving my father. I loved this feeling. I asked him if all his patients experienced this. His response was a long and resounding, "No."

At the end of the hour, we wrapped up our conversation, and on the way out, I said, "I want to get higher." He looked me right in the eyes and said, "Read the Redemption." I had never heard of it before. The only redemption I had ever heard of was a bottle redemption center, where you return your empty bottles in exchange for a nickel or dime each.

So, my next assignment was to figure out what he meant by "Read the Redemption." I was thinking, "This therapy thing is weird and cool. The therapist gives me hints and assignments to figure out." I had no idea what was to come.

My third session was coming up in a few days, and I had no luck finding "The Redemption." This was before search engines were readily available as they are today. It seemed like it was a religious term. I looked in a bible that had come with my house. I was not able to find it in there. It seemed like a spiritual thing, and I thought, *A Course in Miracles* may have a reference to it. I looked in the front glossary, and there it was, in chapter 13, "The Fear of Redemption."

I had finally found my homework assignment. I went into the great room of the house. I relaxed into the brown leather couch and read my current assignment. As I read, I felt that peace again. The more I read, the more inner peace and lightness I felt. I became at one with the words and the pages of the book. I was so relaxed; I didn't even notice that I was leaving my body.

I noticed the back of my head, my shoulders, my hips, my legs. I was still seeing through my physical eyes, but I saw, emerging from my seated body, a version of myself made of an almost-solid, pure white light. I was about to step out of my body completely, when I had a vision of my family coming into the room seeing me lying dead on the couch. I then snapped out of this state. I looked at the book and threw it across the room. I was sucked back into my body and yelled the F word about seven times. I didn't know how out-of-body or near-death experiences worked, but I wanted to cover my bases, and I figured that God would not take me if I said,

"Fuck!" enough times, right? I was in territory that I had no knowledge or ideas about. For such an impactful experience, I had no idea what to make of it.

I had no idea if what just happened was possible, yet I experienced it. I can only describe it as having a million orgasms, if such a thing is even possible. My body was vibrating in a way that I had never felt before. My head was humming with a frequency I had never heard before. I had just gotten higher, and all I could think was, "Holy shit!"

I wasn't going to call the therapist, thinking he might think I'm crazy, so I called Sandra J, the medium, who warned me of what was occurring. Fortunately, she answered her phone. I said, "I figured out the meaning of life and had an out-of-body experience." Her reply was, "What are you talking about?" My response was, "You know exactly what I'm talking about." She laughed and asked, "Is your head humming?" I replied, "Like a tuning fork." She responded, "You better bring that energy down, or you'll take off again." She later became a mentor and friend. I now see this out-of-body experience as more of a near-death experience. I knew in the moment, that I had a choice to stay or go.

My homework assignment was completed, leaving me with more questions than answers. I was on a natural high that I had never felt before; greater even than the day I forgave my father. I could not come down. The humming was constant, and my brain felt as though all its synapses were lit up like a Christmas tree.

I was still working at the flower shop and asked people around me if they knew anything about what I had experienced the day before. I was mostly met with looks of, "What are you talking about? Are you okay?" Both of which implied the question, "Are you crazy?"

After the out-of-body/ near-death experience, my intuition became heightened. People would come into the flower shop, and I could sense their deceased family members. I tactfully asked the customers if they felt comfortable talking about what I was experiencing. Surprisingly they were all interested and open to this confirmation that a deceased loved one was with them. These descriptions and details of their relationships and the messages that I shared were all acknowledged and confirmed by the customers. I had somehow connected to the other side. Now I was the medium. My family, including my wife, were not impressed, and asked me to stop. They said, "It could hurt business." They thought I was crazy, and they lacked any interest in what had happened or what I was experiencing.

Now it was time for my third appointment with Larry R, the therapist. I walked into the office and said, "I don't know if I should thank you or be angry with you." His reply was, "What are you talking about?" I said, "When I was leaving the office at our last session, I stated that, 'I want to get higher.' Your reply was, 'Read the redemption.'"

He said, "I never told you to read the redemption." I said, "You know what? I know what I heard. I didn't know what the redemption was. I believe that you think you didn't say it and I believe that you were somehow used to say the words to me." He asked, "Do you have good teachers around you?" I replied, "Yes, I have three who have had similar experiences as mine, who now teach from this awareness." He responded, "Good because this is far beyond anything I know about."

That was the end of my therapy sessions with Larry R. I had no idea that therapy could be that easy, and that lifechanging. I was finally sane and my family and friends and employees thought I was crazy. The truth is, when a person has an experience like I had, some people cannot relate to it. It seems easier to write the person off as weird, than to explore and understand the experience the person had with compassion and curiosity. In my situation, I went from "normal" to "natural," in a short time. I changed, without giving a memo to my wife, friends, family, or employees. Within a short time, I had unknowingly uncovered and cleared out that which had been veiled in fear for many years.

This profound experience fueled my interest in the mind, body, and spirit, and the connections thereof. I considered myself a self-help junkie before this event. Now it's rare that I find new insights in a book from the self-help genre. Yet, I am always open to learning.

You may be wondering what makes me an expert in fatherhood. The answer is, I'm an expert in raising my son. I'm not an expert in raising yours.

*A Course in Miracle (ACIM)* is my go-to reference guide. My major influences are Eckhart Tolle, author of *The Power of Now*, and Marianne Williamson, who lectures based on the teachings of ACIM around the world. I can listen to them all day long. There are so many great truth tellers and seekers out there. There are also as many, if not many more, who miss the mark.

Hopefully, after reading this book, you will have the awareness to know the difference.

In 2015 I attended the Gestalt International Study Center in Wellfleet, Massachusetts. A rigorous eight-month coaching program, focusing on a process of bringing awareness to our clients using the Gestalt Core Concepts. Some amazing things happened while enrolled in this program, which I will share later. I received my coaching certification in May of 2015 and began my coaching practice soon after.

Currently in 2021, I'm enrolled in *Miracle Minded Coaching*, with Marianne Williamson and her amazing team of coaches, editors, and support staff. At Difference Press, the publishing house at The Author Incubator, the team is headed by Dr. Angela Lauria and her vice president Ramses Rodriguez, along with the amazing editors, publishers, coaches, and support staff. These courses have expanded my awareness in so many ways. Allowing me to experience and coach "awareness" in a deeper, more expansive, and compassionate way. I'm able and encouraged to use my intuitive skills in guiding my clients to experience their inner peace, happiness, and awareness in their relationships with themselves and others.

You're probably wondering why I'm telling you these stories and how they can help you? From my experience, you've most likely experienced some weird phenomenon in your life to some degree. An inexplicable experience is easily forgotten if it doesn't fit your personal narrative. A shocking paradigm shift can either hold you back or help you to grow. There is probably nothing a coaching client can say that will shock me. I've helped people work through trauma, anxiety, depression, weight loss, and even becoming a medium. When people ask me, "What do you do?" I ask them, "What do you hope to have, be, and do in your life and what is holding you back? What will it cost you if you do not remove this block?" I facilitate breakthroughs and "Aha!" moments.

# 3

# TRUTH IS SOMETIMES STRANGER THAN FICTION

B y this point, you are probably wondering where I'm taking you with all these stories. You may be thinking to yourself, "This guy is either crazy, or he may have something that can help me." Perhaps you might even be thinking, "What does this have to do with being a better parent?" Well, it has a lot to do with it. In the book *Finding Flow*, by Mihaly Csikszentmihalyi, the author talks about how intuition is a result of, and is of major importance to, being in a state of "flow." Some other terms related to flow are the zone, mindfulness, consciousness, and awareness.

Before I share this story, I'd like to thank Mary Anne Walk for allowing me to tell it to the world. For much of Mary Anne's career, she was the head of Human Resources of AT&T, worldwide. For the past fifteen years, she has been one of the founding members and assistant director at The Gestalt International Study Center in Wellfleet, Massachusetts. She has been Chairman of the board, and the head of coaching during this time. She also had a successful executive coaching and consulting business, Walk and

Associates. I was fortunate enough to have her as my coach during the eight-month course at GISC. She recently retired and lives part of her time in Sweden with her partner Anders and part of her time at her home in New Jersey. Most importantly, I'm happy to call her one of my dearest friends.

## RALPH'S STORY

The coaching course that I signed up for at GISC is considered one of the best in the country. There were ten students in my class from diverse backgrounds. We were divided into two groups of five. I was put in Mary Anne's group. The other five were put with the other coach Dr. John S, a practicing family therapist. They were a great team and worked well together. There were therapists, human resource directors, health care providers and more in our diverse group of professionals. All were there to develop their coaching skills, using the GISC Core Concepts and Behaviors. I showed up as a florist, with a business and financial background. I felt like I was surrounded by professionals who were out of my league to say the least.

On the first day we were asked to tell the group about ourselves. We were in a semi-circle, and I was the last to be called upon. I listened to everyone's stories and accomplishments. I was the last of ten to speak, Mary Anne called upon me and asked, "Why are you here, and what do you hope to get from the course?" I froze, felt and saw this darkness leave my body. I heard Mary Anne call on me, as she asked me why I was here. I felt like I was not even there, I didn't know what I was saying to her.

When I was done answering the question, I leaned over to the person to my right and asked, "Did I answer the question that I was asked, and did it come across well?" She replied, "You did fine."

The course was set up as three five-day sessions, spread out over eight months.

The days were broken up in two modules. The mornings were for content and concept learning. The afternoons were practicums. These were practice sessions in which we learned to coach and be coached. We were taught deep listening, asking powerful open-ended questions, and reflective listening, among other tools to be used in our practice.

On the third night there, a group of six of us decided to drive to Provincetown at the end of Cape Cod. It was about a half hour drive from the Center, and it was Halloween. P Town, as it is called, is known for being one of the gayest communities in the country. Halloween removed any taboos and inhibitions. It was hilarious, irreverent, and incredibly creative.

We had reservations at an Italian restaurant at seven and we all walked in on time. We ordered our meals and enjoyed each other while also getting to know each other more. I was talking with Laura, a course mate whom I sat next to. After we had settled in and ordered our food, I casually said, "I do readings," Laura asked, "How do you do it?" I said, "Do you want me to give you a reading?" She said that she would like that. I asked her to let me hold something metal that she had been wearing for a while (this is called psychometry). She gave me a bracelet and I immediately talked about her relationship with her sister and mother. I knew names and the dynamics that were involved in their interactions. She seemed to be quite fascinated in what was happening, as well as inquisitive as to how I was able to do it.

A few of the others at the table heard our interaction as well. We then finished dessert, settled with the waiter, and headed back to our hotels. We had two more days left in these first of three, five-day modules. It is not a course you want to go to tired or hungover. We were home by ten to get a restful sleep.

The next day we did the same routine, morning learning and afternoon practicums. It was my turn to be the coach. I was coaching Jennifer. We faced each other. One group member was assigned to critique the twenty-minute session, while the others only observed. We all were able to give feedback after the person assigned to critique was finished. About five minutes into my session with Jennifer, I looked at her, and she had transformed into a mass of flowing tubes of bright light. The mass was about fifty percent larger than Jennifer and was all interconnected and undulating. It's difficult to describe, but it reminded me of the rings of a model atom, but the tubes were too close together to see a nucleus or see through the tangle. It had flowing and undulating florescent tubes of different thicknesses curling back in on themselves, similar to a sphere of spaghetti, but the tubes had no visible endpoints. It was all made of pure, solid, white light. I could hear her talking, yet I was distracted by what I was seeing.

I had never seen anything like this, in this form, before. I stopped the session, looked at my coach, Mary Anne, and told her what had just happened. Mary Anne replied, "Steve, don't say things like this, unless you mean it." I replied, "Oh, I mean it! It's what I saw." I continued the session with Jennifer, like nothing had happened. I now saw her as everyone saw her, as a non-luminous person with a very human body. That was the only time I had that experience. My true feeling is that I saw her as she truly was – a divine being of awareness. This was our fourth day and reservations were made for us all to go to a South African restaurant up the road. All but two people came. Mary Anne decided to come and said that she rarely, if ever goes out with her students, but said she felt a connection with this group. We were seated at one long table; there were ten of us all facing one another. I was facing Becky and Lauren was to my right. We ordered drinks and I was having a conversation with Becky. About twenty minutes into our gathering, I heard Barbara out of my right ear, announce to the whole group, that I do readings. I remember my eyes opening widely at Becky, hers did too, knowing what I could do from the night before. Laura said to the group, "Yeah! Steve does readings. He holds on to a metal object and can tell you all about yourself and what is happening in your life."

I had never done anything like this in front of a group on command. With Becky and I looking at each other in wide-eyed surprise, I heard Mary Anne, who was sitting down and across at the end of the table, yell out in her Arkansas accent, "Maybe he'll get my deceased husband!" She was sending her watch down the table for me to do a reading. Before I could do or say anything, I stood up. I saw the watch coming toward me, and to this day I'm not sure if I touched the watch before I spoke. Looking back now, I must have.

I said to the group, "Who's Ralph?" Mary Anne slapped her hand down on the table and shouted from the far end of the table, "That's my deceased husband!" Ralph had a lot to say, and I was a conduit for him to do so. While all this was happening, I could hear comments like, "What the fuck?" and "Holy shit!" and "What is he doing?" Mary Anne then shouted down the table to me, "I've asked him to find me a man!"

Ralph came through with even more to say. "I have! He looks like Joe Garagiola." Some at the table began Googling this person. He was a famous baseball player and Joe became a regular host on the Today Show. Ralph and Mary Anne connected. It was loving, and the information all resonated with Mary Anne. I'm not sure how long it lasted, maybe ten minutes.

When I do this, my thoughts and personality must step aside to allow their loved ones to connect without my personality interfering. While I don't always recall the whole conversations. I do get bits and pieces. The session wrapped up and there were tears in both Mary Anne's eyes and mine. Mary Anne and I developed a unique connection, for sure. After dinner, Mary Anne and I shared a big hug and she thanked me.

The next morning, Mary Anne announced to the whole group, "What you witnessed last night cannot be taught. It's a unique gift that Steve has." Then she spoke to me and said, "This gift will be helpful in your coaching practice. How we can help you at the Center, is through our coaching methods and the Gestalt core concepts.

As soon as we took our mid-morning break, Mary Anne came over to me and asked if I would be able to teach her to do what I did last evening. I thought it was funny because just a couple of hours earlier, she told the class it was a gift that cannot be taught. I told her I would be happy to teach her. Mary Anne said, "Okay, after you graduate, we'll talk. I'm your coach and it would not be appropriate for you to coach me at the same time." Seven months later, I graduated the course. We had a small ceremony; we were given our certificates of completion and were sent on our way. I hung back until most everyone had left.

I walked up to Mary Anne and asked if she was still interested in being coached to develop her intuition. She replied, "Yes." We went to the lobby and sat at a table. She then said, "What do you charge?" I replied, "Not enough," with a smile.

She replied, "How about a thousand dollars for five sessions?" I said, "That works." (My first paying client.) I then asked her, "On a scale of one to ten, how do you rate your intuition?" She replied, "I'm a solid seven." I replied, "That's pretty high. So, you want to be a Ten?" She replied, "Yes." This was my first opportunity to use The Game of Ten with a paying client. This was the beginning of another long story, and you will understand why when I share the results of my coaching sessions with Mary Anne, and The Game of Ten method, later in the book.

## WHAT TO EXPECT

In the following chapters, you will learn some basic concepts for understanding how you and others think and feel. As a parent, do you feel having more intuition and awareness can prove to be helpful? This is a mindset training book. You can take away as much or as little as you choose. I promise you will not become a medium like I (Steve) did if you don't desire to. I also promise, you will be given the tools to practice a mindset of clarity and peace. Applying the concepts and tools that you are about to read, will not only make you a better parent, but will also make you a better partner, friend, leader, communicator and, I'll say it, a better lover.

So, I ask you to keep an open mind and test out the concepts and tools that you will learn. You don't have to believe or disbelieve what you will be reading, just enjoy, and have a "What if it's true?" mindset.

It is also important to notice your thoughts, feelings and emotions that may arise when learning these concepts. You may experience resistance. If you feel it, you're doing great. Lean into them and allow. It's your mind letting go of past conditioning and beliefs. Don't be afraid. You can always go back to your familiar old thought patterns. We're betting that you won't.

In Chapter 4, you will learn about The Game Often Played: one to nine. This game explains how most people live their lives. There are good days and bad, highs and lows, likes and dislikes, happy points, and sad ones. The Game Often Played is a mindset of duality. It is the human belief that "nobody is perfect, yet I have to be perfect." It is a function of your mind that criticizes you like all the authority figures that helped to shape and mold your thoughts, concepts, and behaviors. In The Game Often Played, you play out the lies you were taught about yourself. You'll do the craziest things to right these wrongs throughout your life, until you overcome The Game often Played using the tools we will provide in this book, or through experience, study, or with the help and guidance of a professional therapist or coach.

In Chapter 5, you will be shown a different approach to understanding how your mind works, and we will explain how your thoughts about yourself, others, and situations, shape your perceptions and experiences. "The more positive your thoughts are, the happier you will be in life." It seems to be a common belief, and it is true in one sense, yet it is phrased by some in a way which ignores external factors like health and poverty. You may be a proficient positive thinker, yet you can never be in alignment with your full potential of awareness until you let go of the duality of positive and negative thinking and move into the level of conscious awareness.

In Chapter 6, you will delve deeper into awareness and what causes you to resist it. You will learn to observe your thoughts, feelings, and emotions to be able to see your part in what you are experiencing in your life and the lives of others. You will begin the transformative work of moving from a fear-based mindset to a love-based mindset.

In Chapter 7 you will read some incredible stories and results those clients have had while using The Game of Ten process. You will learn the theory behind this tool as well as the benefits that you will experience when using this tool in parenting and daily living.

In Chapter 8 you will learn the rules, definitions, and terminologies of The Game of Ten. You will learn how to play this game and integrate it into your life. You will journey from normal to natural, a fear-based mindset to a love-based one. You will learn and hopefully experience a new mindset in alignment with more universal truths, as opposed to the illusions created by the mind.

In Chapter 9 you will learn the practical usage of The Game of Ten and how to assimilate this new mindset into your daily life. "It's not difficult, it's different." You will understand that this mindset is a practice – a process, rather than an event. It's a journey of untangling the misinformation and misunderstandings from your past conditioning.

Enjoy the journey to awareness. There are many people in this world who can support you along the way.

4

## THE GAME OFTEN PLAYED

I n this chapter you will be introduced to The Game Often Played. After which, you will be introduced to The Game of Ten, a set of principles for viewing the world through love and awareness, which we believe to be the natural human state, insofar as such a thing exists. You will see how your thoughts affect your perceptions about the world you live in. You will understand that your thoughts affect your emotions and the importance of being aware of your thoughts, feelings, and emotions.

While your emotions are physical reactions, caused by changes in neurotransmitter and hormone levels within the brain, feelings are the conscious experience of these emotional reactions. The mind emerges from the body and is influenced by it, but the body is also influenced by the actions of the brain and the processes of the mind it gives rise to. Mindset can be the difference between a runaway positive cycle of improvement, and a downward spiral of fear, suffering, and illness.

## AMANDA'S STORY

I had a client, Amanda M., whom I first met at a social gathering. I mentioned to her that I was working with clients with anxiety and depression. A few days after our meeting, she called me and expressed an interest in the anxiety portion of my coaching. I had her fill out a questionnaire (mine is called a discovery form) to find out where she was, so to speak, with her anxiety.

According to her written responses from her discovery form, she was at a solid level of eight. This said to me that she had only minor feelings of anxiety or depression. Two steps away from Ten, where there is no space for lasting anxiety or depression. As we began the session, I said that it seemed her anxiety was likely at a bearable level, that according to her discovery form, she was functioning at a consistent level of eight.

To clarify, I asked, "So, on a scale of one to ten, when it comes to anxiety, you are operating at eight?" There was a pause, and she replied, "I'm really a four and a half." She said she felt stuck and did not know why. She went on to tell me that she did energy work, breathing classes, and had a good understanding of mental health. She always felt great after the classes, yet the next morning she would once again find herself battling with anxiety.

She then said, "I don't know why." I responded, "Were you ever told by yourself, or another person, that it is okay not to know why?" She had never looked at it like that before. Now things were making sense to her. Her revelation of being separate from Ten by five and a half points was a good place to start.

Letting go of the guilt and shame for her "not knowing

why," helped in her willingness to trust this process. I asked her if she was open to having an experimental visualization. She agreed and we began the process. I explained to her that to be a four and a half, with regards to anxiety, there must be a depletion of fifty-five percent of her energy from herself. I asked her if she felt her anxiety as being outside of her. She replied, "Yes, it feels like I'm beside myself looking at myself." I replied, "You are, in a way." Then I asked if she was ready to get started. She was, and we began. I asked Amanda to see that energy outside of her as "divine energy" that gets pushed out by negative thoughts, feeling and emotions. It is trying to get back in, but it's blocked by this resistant pressure.

The stage was set to begin the visualization. First, we had to change the paradigm. Anxiety was no longer anxiety. It was going to be called another name more fitting to the truth. Amanda decided to call it "Beautiful Love." I asked Amanda to envision herself in a spacious clear tube, open at the bottom and the top. She said that it felt uncomfortable to have the bottom open. I explained the Beautiful Love had to have a way back in and this will be the way. She agreed and we moved on. I asked Amanda to describe this Beautiful Love. She said it was purple liquid, more viscous than water. I asked her for more details. She replied, "It is bright and glittery."

I said, "Amanda, you are standing in a spacious clear tube, in a never depleting spring of this Beautiful Love. This Beautiful Love that is beside you flows into the spring. You are up above knees in this Beautiful Love at four and a half. It is stuck at four and a half. You look down to your side and there is a release valve. Do you see it?"

Amanda replied, "Yes."

I asked, "What kind of valve is it?"

She replied, "It is a round spigot valve, like when you turn off a hose."

"Are you all set to begin?" I asked.

Amanda replied, "Yes."

I replied, "Whenever you feel comfortable, you can turn on the spigot."

Amanda decided to open the spigot all the way. We carried on in general conversation. After a few minutes, I checked in as to how the Beautiful Love was doing. Amanda said, "It's at six." She said it felt good and she was comfortable at six and was keeping the spigot open. We continued talking about other happenings in her life. Within another few minutes, I checked in and she said she was now at eight. I let her know that she controls the spigot and that she can take a break at any time. I also explained that if she brings this Beautiful Love up to Ten that it can overflow and go back into the infinite spring. Within three minutes, Amanda said, "I'm at Ten and it's overflowing."

"Great," I said.

There was silence as Amanda breathed gently and enjoyed the Beautiful Love flowing through her once again. Amanda's anxiety was finally gone. She had turned it into Beautiful Love. I explained that she could use this visualization tool whenever she felt what she would have called anxiety, and now calls Beautiful Love, asking to come back in.

It has been said that holding onto thoughts of the past leads to feelings of depression, and holding onto thoughts of the future leads to feelings of anxiety. You have the illusionary ability to give your power away to a person or situation. When you do this, it creates a void which your conditioned mind will fill with fear. It will give you the illusion that your power has been taken from you, that your power is outside of your control. People and situations will come into your life to validate this mindset and use it against you. Your fearful mind thinks there is something to be dreaded, and to be avoided at all costs. Often, it doesn't even know what the dreaded event is.

## WHAT IS THE CONDITIONED MIND?

You think your thoughts perfectly describe reality. The truth is, they are a creation of the conditioned mind. Thoughtless awareness of perception (sight, smell, etc.) is the best human approximation of reality. Observing thoughts derived from present moment awareness is as close to what is real as thoughts can bring you, and as close to awareness as the conditioned mind will ever experience. Yet, though you can be aware of thoughts, thoughts are not awareness.

You were born with an unconditioned mind (all nature, no nurture yet). Through conditioning, you practiced, accepted, and internalized certain patterns and behaviors instead of others. The most noticeable and most complex of these patterns and behaviors is thought. Your conditioned mind builds structures, patterns, and thought forms from awareness (which is formless) because your conditioned mind thinks your awareness needs support. It does not.

Comparisons drive the conditioned mind. The conditioned mind deals in duality, opposites, degrees, and polarities. The most common and destructive judgements are, what is right? What is enough? First comes the personalization of a thought: "*I think*," then comes emotional attachment to that thought: "*I feel*."

## HOW DO THOUGHTS AFFECT YOU?

The separate mind, or at least the illusion of it, is mentioned in many world religions. Indeed, we would be remiss for not mentioning the contributions of Taoist and Buddhist philosophy to humanity's study of the mind and our search for contentment. This concept of the separate mind was also depicted in Genesis, when Adam and Eve defied God by eating from the tree of the knowledge of good and evil. In the story, they were then exiled from Eden.

Some ideas about a separate mind are contained within the loaded concept of "free will." The ability to choose for oneself, essentially to think thoughts "against nature." You can look at your mind as a supercomputer running a program called "awareness." There is, however, usually another program at play: thinking, which includes worrying, planning, daydreaming, and analyzing. Thoughts run somewhat independently from awareness, although thoughts consume the limited field of view, or attention span, which awareness has to use. Thoughts are quite different between people, but we can assume that the quality, (qualia) of awareness, feels rather similar between humans with similar brains. A mind consumed by thoughts seems to forget awareness exists, whereas a mind in a state of complete awareness has no use for distracting thoughts. When a person thinks about "I, me, myself" and begins to create a self-image and identity within their mind, which their thinking mind both protects in some situations and attacks in others, we call this the ego. This engrained process of self-identification, worry, unawareness, and reactivity, can be thought of as The Game Often Played. Despite the name, it isn't enjoyable.

The ego wants its illogical thoughts and feelings to seem logical, and therefore real and important. But when you question the assumptions beneath judgmental or painful thoughts and worries, you weaken the ego's power enormously.

One linguistic hurdle in this book is the definition and use of the term *thought* in modern English when compared to its usage by ACIM, Tolle, and ourselves. Some consider awareness a form of thought, some consider all activities of the mind, even unconscious ones, to be forms of thought. Some see both creativity and worrying as part of the same concept of thought.

To us, thought is the internal dialogue of judgmental feelings, voices, or images. Imaginings can be thoughts, but they emerge from different systems than verbal thoughts, so it's possible for someone to be tormented by one type of thought, such as verbal thoughts, but be unbothered by imagined images. Einstein's "thoughts of God," (laws of the universe) are clearly very different from your thoughts of "What's for dinner tonight?"

It is consistently astonishing and must be re-emphasized that many of the concepts we arrived at are found or hinted at in other teachings and methods. It says that we are likely on the right path, and that we can potentially contribute to the conversation.

That we are right with the awareness we have, and that awareness aligns with some of the greatest teachers throughout history, is a good indicator that we (and you) are aware, and on the right path to awareness.

You are never disconnected from awareness. When you are operating from thought, you "think" you are separate from the peace of awareness, and indeed you may not feel peaceful at all. We call this separation from awareness: The Game Often Played.

From The Game Often Played, you operate in duality. Most thoughts are of the past or future (and even present thoughts are based on past conditioning). You cannot be present in the moment, especially when so many repetitive and negative thoughts consume your attention. When your awareness is clouded by these thoughts, feelings, and emotions, you project them onto other people and situations in your life.

If you are looking to change your life from this mindset of past thought and future worries, you're going to have a difficult time. A common saying, though one certainly not coined by a psychologist or dice-enthusiast is: "The definition of insanity is doing the same thing over and over and expecting different results." This is exactly what is happening in The Game Often Played.

The illusion of separation from awareness and connectedness is essential for you to play this game. The main motivator in The Game Often Played is fear. Perhaps you've heard the acronym: False Evidence Appearing Real. This is true. Many people go about their lives playing The Game Often Played; truly believing that they are independent, self-made, and individual. The fact is that you are and always will be *interdependent* with others and the world around you.

Stephen Covey mentions the Game-Theory terms, Win-Win, Win-Lose, Lose-Lose and No Deal, in his book, *Seven Habits of Highly Effective People.* When playing The Game Often Played, your mind believes that there must be a loser and a winner, or no winners at all. As a result of this zero-sum-game mentality, you lose, and everyone loses. It is a mindset based on fear and fearful thoughts.

Awareness guides you with love, and leads to win-win or no-deal outcomes. This is a fundamental difference between The Game of Ten, and The Game Often Played. Do you see where we're going with this and how it relates to being an amazing parent? Being aware of which game you are playing is important. Are you parenting from love or from fear? As a person, parent, partner, or community member, indeed, in any given situation, this awareness is essential for making informed choices in life.

Awareness is the key difference between the two games that are being played. One game is real, the other an illusion. You can probably guess which one is which. The Game Often Played runs on a program of thought, fear, and self-identification with things and ideas. You can look at this as though its operating system is based in fear and all thoughts, feelings, and are emotions derived from fear. It is based on body identification rather than 'being' identification. Your body will tell you when you are in this program with pain and suffering both physically and emotionally.

Your thoughts about anything and everything (fill in the blank), will be based on fear to some extent. They will find a home in your body and express themselves as pain, discomfort and eventually dis-ease. This mental process has been called the ego, unconscious mind, narcissist, saboteur, the imposter, the mind made self and yes, even the devil. The good news for you is that it's not real. It wants you to *believe* it is real at all costs, because it believes that it is you, and that you (it) will die if the belief and fear stops. I assure you that there is and will always be a price to pay when playing The Game Often Played. The price is giving away your power to a person or situation which you perceive to be both different from and outside of yourself.

The moves used within The Game Often Played are guilt, (*"I did something bad"*) and shame, (*"I am bad"*), as well as self-doubt, anger, hate, sadness, fear, and your identification as a body. From mild irritation of your thoughts and feelings and emotions, to severe illness and disease, both physical and mental, all these concepts and experiences originate from fear.

If you are experiencing any of this, let's be clear, we are not saying that you are bad or wrong in any way. I am asking you to look at the thoughts and feelings you are holding on to from the past, and to look at what you are projecting onto the future. Soon you will learn how to release these thoughts, feelings, and emotions that no longer serve your physical, mental, and emotional health and wellbeing.

## THE GAME OFTEN PLAYED©: ONE TO NINE

If you play The Game Often Played, you will never win. You made the game and the rules. The rules were developed and conditioned through all your past thoughts, feelings, and emotions that were fearful or unloving in any way. All these aspects will be used against you while playing this game.

In this chapter, we introduce the antithesis to The Game of Ten®. We will properly introduce The Game of Ten in an upcoming chapter, but this paragraph can offer a brief explanation. The Game of Ten is a set of fundamental assumptions and affirmations, which can be tried out similar to the rules of a game. The Game of Ten gets its name from self-report rating scales numbered from one to ten. The Game of Ten sees a person playing nine as being ninety percent happy, or happy roughly ninety percent of the time. A person playing one would be happy or content roughly ten percent of the time, perhaps less, and uncomfortable or suffering ninety percent of the time or more. While nine is seen as a "positive thinker," Ten is seen as a leap of faith away from nine, in that, reaching Ten means living from complete awareness and acceptance, and living without mental suffering or prolonged fear. Part of playing The Game of Ten means understanding that to see oneself as less-than Ten is actually an illusion. This validates all mental suffering and fear as subjectively real for those playing Off-Ten©, while also asserting that the capacity for awareness and acceptance is already within everyone. You are and always have been Ten. You were and are appointed Ten. Sometimes when you are hooked by the thought about being Off-Ten, in other words, dis-appointed from Ten, you blame other people, things, and situations for your dis-appointment.

## THE RULES OF THE GAME OFTEN PLAYED

The rules of this game are simple yet destructive. They are assumptions masquerading as truth. They create feedback loops of uncertainty, insufficiency, and lack. They are the thoughts which turn fear into worry, hatred, and suffering:

I am not Ten.

You/ we/ they are not Ten.

I am not right with the awareness I have.

They are not right with the awareness they have.

I am not doing the best I can with the awareness I have.

They are not doing the best they can with the awareness they have.

I am not enough.

You/ we/ they are not enough.

I don't do enough.

You/ we/ they don't do enough.

I don't have enough.

You/ we/ they don't have enough.

It can happen in a split second. The moment you think or believe one or more of these statements, you take yourself Off-Ten. The more Off-Ten thoughts or beliefs you hold, the further away from Ten you feel, and the more guilt and shame you have around these thoughts and feelings. Bringing your thoughts, feelings, and emotions to awareness is essential to releasing them. Being Off-Ten is situational. From Off-Ten, you get mad, sad, and scared, and take it out on others, or yourself, or both. You might say that you become temporarily insane and willing to share this insanity with others or to further inflict it upon yourself.

The Game Often Played is the basis for all your perceptions and judgements of all that's not right with your world. Take a look and see if any of the assumptions of The Game Often Played pass through your mind at any time. When you hold these assumptions, your world is insane, not right, and people, situations, and organizations are not, don't do, or don't have enough [fill in the blank] to make things right, enough, or Ten. It all seems quite sane for you to complain about, accuse, and condemn others for being insufficient or being too much. Indeed, loud condemnation can bring awareness to issues and lead to improvement, but rather than attributing responsibility and enacting change, The Game Often Played is fundamentally a fearful, judgmental, and hateful state of mind. When you play The Game Often Played, you see the quite subjective emotional concepts of good, bad, and enough, as objective, and use these arbitrary judgements against yourself and others.

The problem arises when the individual or group doing the complaining about real issues, feels guilt and shame for thinking about it, judging it as wrong, and judging that they aren't doing enough. When you are Off-Ten, people, things, and situations are either always too much or never quite enough. Too much of a bad thing and not enough of a good thing can both be seen as undesirable and lacking. You will always be looking for, wanting, and needing more or less of something. Wanting and needing create a monotonous and vicious cycle which can only end when the cycle is unconditioned. This requires you to transmute the mental state of needing and lacking, into a mental state of preferring, choosing, and accepting yourself and your life as it is right now. Obviously, some people are starving or poor or abused or wrongfully imprisoned. Some people legitimately do not have enough of what they need to survive or thrive. The Game of Ten is meant to help people thrive emotionally once they do have enough resources and support to survive and thrive physically, and it may be sooner than they think. The Game of Ten also asserts that everyone is doing the best they can with the awareness they have, and with the physical or perceived constraints of the world around them. Few people suffer by choice. Most suffer by unawareness and by terrible circumstances. It's charming to say that everyone intrinsically has enough, but to help others find enough materially and emotionally is far more impactful and rewarding.

## THE GAME OFTEN PLAYED: ONE TO THREE

If you are behaving from this realm, between one and three out of Ten, things seem quite bleak. You seem to have little hope that things will change for the better. You are a victim of what was, and what is happening to you. The conditioned mind, with its negativity bias (assigning greater significance to events perceived to be bad), hates, yet loves this position. It is the mindset of highest resistance to what is real.

The Game of Ten is a framework for finding relief from harmful thought patterns once your material needs are met at a basic level. An advantage to relief from harmful thought patterns is that it will usually help you to meet your material needs in a more effective and healthy way for all. The Game of Ten is not the only requirement for a joyful life of meaning and purpose, but it seems to be a missing piece for many.

Traumatic experiences can lead to an extremely "deep" form of conditioning. Trauma can create lifelong struggles, learned helplessness, attachment disorders, stress disorders, and depressive disorders. It burns fear and pain into the conscious memory, and into the older brain regions and deeper nervous system reserved for unconscious and reflexive response. "It's all in your head" does not invalidate experiences; to those who understand the brain, it validates the experiences. We are nothing if not experiencers, thus personal experience is the best metric by which we can understand the world and how best to respect and help the beings within it.

It is important to realize that a particularly hurtful thought can bring you down to the levels of one, two, or three in an instant. Playing from one feels dark, unsafe, and completely unloving. It is your living hell. When you are in this state of mind, you feel there is nothing that can hurt you more than you have already been hurt. Nothing and no one can disappoint you more than you have already been disappointed. Alternatively, you could simultaneously feel as though you are at rock bottom and feel mortally terrified of sinking even lower. It is a victim's mindset and the stories that you can tell yourself from this mindset will prove to you that it is true. You will seek and find others to buy into your story and you may find that your misery is validated or supported by others who feel like you, if you even feel supported at all.

There is never, or rarely ever, enough. Playing from one, two, or three means constant needing, wanting and complaining. You will take little or no responsibility for your situation or the situations of others. Your responsibility, if there is any responsibility, will be in the form of blaming yourself, or others, or both, often for things beyond your control, rather than accepting responsibility for your actions and understanding the causal roles of other people and dynamics. It is the blame, guilt, and shame game, played at its best.

We'd like to clarify; horrific things happen in this world. We are in no way denying or condoning any of those things. We're also not condoning the victim mindset. It can potentially, over time, be more harmful to a person or group than the horrific and damaging events that occurred in the first place.

If you have been playing this game, you love to share your misery with others. By sharing your guilt, shame, and hurt, there is a temporary relief from carrying that burden all alone. Complaining against the "what is" of the moment, maintains your false sense of superiority and security, because you are right. The rest of the world is wrong (so you believe). It is the ultimate thought pattern of not being, doing, or having enough.

There is a direct correlation between your distance from Ten, and the amount of guilt, shame, fear, and self-doubt you feel and hold on to. These thoughts and feelings reinforce patterns in your mind and body and will impact your actions and cause you to attract a similar level of situations, people, and drama into your life. This feedback loop of ingraining hurtful patterns and attracting harmful situations will keep the player of one to three in a dream of depression, anxiety, disappointment, and victimhood. The Game Often Played began through thinking with the fearful, conditioned mind.

This is a mindset where your negative thoughts, feelings, and emotions are at their worst. Fear and self-doubt become the basis of your existence, leaving you completely lost in your thoughts, feelings, and emotions. Joy, peace, happiness, and love will find others, but never you. In the words of the Wicked Witch of the West as she was melting, "What a world! What a world!"

So now you have an idea of what a one to three looks like. We're sure that you have met a few in your life, or perhaps you recognize these patterns in yourself. The part of The Game of Ten that you may not know is, if you see it, you are it. You may observe one to three behaviors, and if you judge them, or want yourself or another to be different, you resist reality and become Off-Ten.

## THE GAME OFTEN PLAYED: FOUR TO SIX

If you haven't figured it out yet, your level from one to nine is all about the amount and awareness-level of thoughts that you have identified with, both "positive" and "negative." In this arena, four to six, the glass is half-full and half empty, depending on your mindset in each moment and situation. The individual playing four, five, or six, is attached to a balance of positive and negative thinking. As we move away from one and closer to Ten, we become less resistant to the present moment and situation. We wish to emphasize that one to nine, The Game Often Played, is simply a model, and is used to point to behaviors of thought that will create interpretations of the world which seem real but are based entirely on biased and judgmental thoughts.

As you move up to the level of four to six, you will notice

that life will present choices and opportunities that were not seen at one to three. It is important to be aware that we attract at the level from which we are operating and projecting. In other words, fours attract "level-four" people and situations, and sixes attract "level-six" people and situations. This can be described by the "weak manifestation hypothesis." Instead of saying that your thoughts control the fabric of the universe, the weak manifestation hypothesis suggests that through your actions, inactions, and interpretations, you both bring about and perceive situations to be closer to your level of resistance/ awareness in a self-reinforcing cycle.

How you interpret and respond to present events influences not only how you interpret and respond to future events, but also biases your behavior towards bringing about favorable or unfavorable circumstances, based on your level of resistance or acceptance (one to Ten). For example, getting a flat tire while otherwise safe and content, can be seen from Ten as an opportunity to practice installing a spare tire, as well as an opportunity to be thankful that the flat occurred in a safe place to pull over. Such a mindset will also prevent driving-while-Off-Ten on your way home. Road rage never helped anybody achieve joy.

On the other hand, a motorist unable to afford a replacement tire would be more likely to experience fear, anger, and anxiety following a flat, since, in our society, scarce money is a material factor that affects so many facets of one's mental and physical health. In the weak manifestation hypothesis, your material conditions, your mindset, and your actions all reinforce one another. "Gratitude" and "inner peace" cannot fill your stomach or mend your tire, and they should not be forced on anyone, but they can help you to see possibilities, avoid pitfalls, and find contentment where others would not.

Before you judge others, be aware that by the act of

judging them, you've asked for these less-than-Ten situations and people to come into your life. These people and situations are here to teach you to accept them as they are, and to let go of the thoughts, feelings, and judgements about them. This is the concept of *forgiveness*. All thoughts are for-giving (they are meant to be given away, to be let go of). Never be afraid to let go of thoughts. You can always bring them back if they serve you and others. Just remember, the more thoughts, feelings, and emotions that you have which judge or resist "what is," the lower on the one-to-Ten scale you will feel.

Thoughts about yourself and others, that are not unconditionally loving and accepting, are judgmental of yourself and others. Even believing that another person is playing The Game Often Played, is enough to disconnect you from Ten. The disconnect happens when you think that you are your thoughts. You are not your thoughts; you are the awareness that you are having thoughts. Thoughts are a construct of your conditioned mind. The problem occurs when you believe your thoughts to be your "awareness" and yourself. Nothing good can come from believing that your biased and judgmental thoughts represent unbiased and objective truth.

## THE GAME OFTEN PLAYED: SEVEN TO NINE

Here you have the high-functioning "positive" thinkers. If you are playing from seven, eight, or nine, you will see yourself as a generally positive person. You will see life's glass as more than half-full. Most people who are trapped in their thinking minds will see this as a comfortable and acceptable balance of "positive" and "negative" thinking. You know that things could be much worse (you could be playing one to six), and you also know that things could be better. We use the word "could" for a reason. When you believe something *could be better*, you convince yourself that it *is worse*. However far away from Ten you believe yourself to be, you will find yourself consciously or unconsciously expressing guilt and shame. When Off-Ten, you fixate on the perceptions of *not enough* and *too much* within life's situations.

The closer you get to Ten, the closer you get to unconditional love, happiness, and peace. When you're playing seven to nine, you get closer to Ten than others, yet you never quite reach it. There's an old Maine saying when an out of stater asks a local Mainer for directions. The Mainer says, "You can't get there from here!" (Pronounced: get *they-ahh from hee-yuh*) meaning the Mainer believes the route is too difficult or indirect to attempt.

What people often don't realize while stuck Off-Ten, is that happiness will never completely be present in one to nine. Saying "I will be happy when..." is conditional upon some future event which exists only in your imagination. You have placed a condition on the situation in front of you in order for happiness to be accepted and present in your awareness. When trapped in The Game Often Played, it is easier to pretend that you will be happy later, than to admit that you don't have the ability to find happiness in the present moment. Unconditional love, happiness, inner peace, and absolution are experienced from Ten only.

The awareness from nine allows you to empathize with people from one to nine. Most positive thinkers believe that they have reached some endpoint of positive thinking, though many remain dissatisfied, perhaps by definition. This belief (that positive thinking is the end goal) has formed the basis of a *positive thinking movement* in recent decades. When you tell a friend that you went to the store and their reply is a monotone "awesome," do you ever ask yourself: "was it really awesome, or does this person just say that about every-thing and to everyone?"

Reaching Ten is a leap of faith that few will take. It will mean giving up the belief that your thoughts keep you safe, and letting go of the way you think things could, would, and should be. Your egoic, conditioned mind thinks it runs your life. It is not aware of Ten, and a person living from Ten does not concern themselves with what remains of their condi-tioned mind. The conditioned mind thinks it is necessary for your survival. It thinks if you don't need it, it will die, and therefore, it thinks you will die if you let go of it. The only death caused by letting go of the conditioned mind is the death of the power and control it thinks it has over your life. It only controls you if you allow it to, but often it's hard to realize that you have allowed this false sense of self to influ-ence your actions.

You are now beginning to see how important it is to be aware of when your mind is loving and when it is not. You are also likely noticing the positive-negative duality within your current self-talk and state of mind, and the effects that these judgments and assumptions can have on you.


## MEANS AND ENDS

You cannot separate means and ends. Living from Ten requires means and ends to be aligned with one another. *You must live with the mindset you wish to have when your abstract goals have already been achieved.*

Stop deluding yourself that you are "putting off" inner peace for a justifiable reason. Feeling inadequate doesn't give you an edge; it just gives you unhealthy thought patterns that can interfere with your life in many ways. Just because you have lost the awareness of how to get there, doesn't justify dismissing unconditional peace, love, and happiness altogether. True inner peace is not a sense of freedom within a continuous stream of thoughts, but rather it is freedom from being controlled by your thoughts.

Means correspond to the ends. Every moment spent as a means to an end is also an end in itself. If you suffer in all the moments leading up to your goal, then no matter your achievement, one of the results was your own suffering. Ideally, you will become aware of how your present thoughts and actions affect both your present experience, and long-term quality of life. Awareness, happiness, and inner peace are both ends in themselves, and the means by which you can create a life in which every moment is defined by joy rather than suffering.

You must overcome the lie of "I'll be happy *when*" by realizing you can be happy *during*. You have the potential for presence, stillness, and self-awareness in every waking moment. Emotions can come and go while you are in this state. You may not always feel happy or comfortable, even when present, still, and self-aware, but when you maintain this peaceful and observant baseline within your mind, however small it may feel at a given time, it will remind you that you are allowed to be happy before, during, and after anything. In short, you can replace "I'll be happy when..." with "I am content now."

In all projects, indeed all conscious actions, you are working toward near-term and long-term goals. The best way to ensure your long-term goals are achieved, is to ensure your near-term actions and goals are improving your ability to meet your long-term goals. As individuals or groups, we can organize ourselves and our lives in a way that models the future life, mindset, or egalitarian society we wish to create; creating immediate satisfaction regardless of whether the ideal goal is achieved. Your thoughts and behaviors are processes which are either built-up through practice or which atrophy in disuse. You will struggle to find contentment *then* if you are not practicing it *now*.

# 5

# HOW ARE YOU DOING RAISING
# YOUR CHILD?

I n this chapter you will learn more about The Game of
Ten, specifically, you will read about its use within a
coaching session, and you will be asked some questions to better understand what game you are playing. The
stage is being set to explain the principles and demonstrate
the effectiveness of the mindset fostered by The Game of Ten
rather than The Game Often Played. Mindset awareness, or
self-awareness more broadly, will help you to make the
conscious choice to play from Ten.

Everyone is doing the best they can with the awareness
they have. In Robert Sapolsky's book *Behave*, he shows
numerous examples of causal relationships between biology
and subsequent behaviors, ever shrinking the likelihood of
any such thing as "free will" and arguing that we should not
use it as an assumption. It also suggests that everyone is
doing the best they can with the awareness and biology they
have. While we may be unable to use the rhetoric of "self-
control" to "guilt" people into behaving in mutually beneficial ways, we may still be able to change our interpretations
of events, and therefore our reactions to them. By raising

both the quality of awareness itself, and spreading awareness about the facts of the material world, we are able to raise both the degree and the breadth of others' awareness. This awareness includes both their self-awareness and their knowledge of the material world.

This is the goal of awareness-raising activism such as autism awareness, breast cancer awareness, etc. (Acceptance movements must follow awareness movements, just as acceptance follows awareness). We are doing the best we can with the awareness we have, and when we gain greater awareness, more information, we can do even "better" than we otherwise would, so to speak.

## MICHAEL G'S STORY

I had a client I met at a business gathering. I will call him Michael G. We started off with the usual small talk, a standard practice at these types of events. I noticed his name tag and saw that he worked for a large international bank. I asked him about what he did with the bank. He told me that he had a major role in allocating funds for mergers and expanding businesses. After talking about what I do in my business as a mindset coach, Michael agreed to meet with me for lunch.

It turned out that Michael G and I had a lot in common. We read many of the same books and knew of many of the same spiritual and self-help teachers. Names like Eckhart Tolle, Stephen Covey, Dr. Wayne Dyer, Tony Robbins, etc. Michael wore an elastic band on his left wrist. If he ever felt that he wasn't being present, he would snap it to bring his attention back to the present moment. We had about three sessions over a two-month period, after which he decided that he had enough to work with and we were done for the time being.

A couple of months passed, and I had developed The Game of Ten. I was ready to put it into practice with clients. I called Michael and said, "I have something that I feel will be just what you're looking for." I figured that a guy who uses elastic bands to snap himself back to awareness would be willing to try anything. Michael said, "I can't meet. Money is tight. We are putting on a new deck. It's going to be more expensive than planned." My reply was, "I will do the session for free." I wanted to know if The Game of Ten was going to be useful to clients. I knew that Michael would give me the feedback I wanted, a truthful opinion. I started the session by giving Michael a five-page script on The Game of Ten which I had written for a recent presentation. He read it over and looked up at me with a smile. I asked him if he was Ten. His reply was that he was a nine. Still trying to figure out how to use this process, I asked him what it would take to get to Ten. His reply was, "I like being a nine. I need that edge to be better at what I do. It motivates me."

In essence, he was saying that if he was Ten, if he felt truly at peace, there would be no motivation to achieve more. He was right insofar as he would no longer be able to use fear and lack to motivate himself. What Michael did not realize was that he had always had the ability to create a life of enough. I asked him if he could just imagine for a minute that he was Ten. He resisted, saying that he didn't want to, that nine was good enough.

I agreed with him and said, "That's fine." I would accept that his best is nine under one condition. The condition was that I would get to call him Sisyphus, the mythological figure who was sentenced to push a giant boulder up a mountain for eternity for his arrogance and deceit. When almost reaching the top of the hill, the enchanted boulder would overwhelm him and roll back to the base of the mountain.

Michael did not like the comparison. We began a stare down of silence. It may have only lasted a couple of minutes, yet it was a long couple of minutes. Michael broke the silence by saying that I was an "asshole!" Then he said, "I'm a Ten." My response was, "You can be any number you choose. It's always up to you." That was the end of our session. We had lunch and never mentioned payment for the session. After lunch, we both stood up and, to my surprise, Michael grinned and handed me my full hourly rate.

My comparison of Michael to Sisyphus was spot on. Being less than Ten is the most arrogant and self-aggrandizing thing that you can claim. The Game Often Played uses delusional assumptions to justify your misery. You think that you are better than Ten even when you are actually playing small and Off-Ten.


## THE GAME OF TEN DISCOVERY FORM

Below is a discovery form I send to clients to fill out before we begin working together and our coaching agreement has been established. If you do not want to write in this book, you can download the discovery form for free on my website, OverTheLookingGlass.com, or write your answers on a separate sheet of paper.

Please fill out this form and circle the number that best fits how you are feeling now, or how you've been feeling recently. This survey is to provide insight into your thoughts and feelings, where you are feeling stuck, and how you may be able to help yourself. There are no right or wrong feelings or answers. Go with the number you feel after reading the question without overthinking it. If you feel the need to explain, please do so. Explanations are optional. One is "not likely at all," and ten is "extremely likely." Along with your present experience, consider your thoughts, feelings, emotions, and behaviors from the last day, week, or month.

1. How likely are you to accept yourself as you are now?
1 2 3 4 5 6 7 8 9 10
Feel free to explain why you chose this number.

2. How likely are you to accept other people or situations as they are now?
1 2 3 4 5 6 7 8 9 10
Feel free to explain why you chose this number.

3. How likely are you to feel that you are doing the best you can with the awareness you have?
1 2 3 4 5 6 7 8 9 10
Feel free to explain why you chose this number.

4. How likely are you to feel that others are doing the best they can with the awareness they have?
1 2 3 4 5 6 7 8 9 10
Feel free to explain why you chose this number.

5. How likely are you to feel that you are enough?
1 2 3 4 5 6 7 8 9 10
Feel free to explain why you chose this number.

6. How likely are you to feel that others are enough?
1 2 3 4 5 6 7 8 9 10
Feel free to explain why you chose this number.

7. How likely are you to feel that you do enough?
1 2 3 4 5 6 7 8 9 10
Feel free to explain why you chose this number.

8. How likely are you to feel that others do enough?

1 2 3 4 5 6 7 8 9 10

Feel free to explain why you chose this number.

9. How likely are you to feel that you have enough?

1 2 3 4 5 6 7 8 9 10

Feel free to explain why you chose this number.

10. How likely are you to feel that others have enough?

1 2 3 4 5 6 7 8 9 10

Feel free to explain why you chose this number.

11. How likely are you to graciously accept a compliment?

1 2 3 4 5 6 7 8 9 10

Feel free to explain why you chose this number.

12. Given the opportunity, how likely are to give a compliment with sincerity?

1 2 3 4 5 6 7 8 9 10

Feel free to explain why you chose this number.

13. How likely are you to let go of the negative feelings from your past?

1 2 3 4 5 6 7 8 9 10

Feel free to explain why you chose this number.

14. How likely are you to be at peace with the future?

1 2 3 4 5 6 7 8 9 10

Feel free to explain why you chose this number.

After filling out this form, add up your score and divide it by fourteen. This will give you an idea of how you see yourself on a scale of one to ten at this moment and will give insight into how you see yourself as a parent. Wherever you reported less than ten, you have room for improvement. The higher the score, the more awareness and contentment you have on this particular topic. Awareness is the key to your happiness in any situation. You have likely noticed many repeating themes as we lead up to The Game of Ten.

Did you notice that six of the questions have to do with the concept of "enough?" Enough is the quantity of contentment, awareness, and Ten. It is quite different from the subjective and egoic judgments of "not enough" or "too much." The only place experienced from awareness is "here." The only time experienced from awareness is "now." The mind has distorted the already imagined concepts of past and future through thought, self-identity, worry, and regret. *Be Enough Here Now*.

Giving and receiving compliments can demonstrate how you think about giving and receiving more generally. Are you receiving enough from yourself and others? Are you able to share this *enough* with yourself and others? How do you respond to receiving compliments? Do you marginalize them or deflect them? Giving and receiving must be in alignment before you experience abundance. Many people are great at giving compliments but bad at receiving them because they both wish to express love toward everyone, and don't believe anyone could love or appreciate them, if they even love themselves.

Awareness is the key to knowledge. Knowledge can only be obtained through awareness. What we think, is often subjective, emotional, or reductive, and it may or may not be the truth. Awareness is the closest we come to experiencing truth, as awareness is humanity's purest form of experiencing reality. With more awareness, we get closer to the truth. Awareness of the self can be deepened through mindfulness and practice. Awareness of the world can be broadened and deepened by research and experience. It is important to see everyone as doing the best they can and right (as correct as possible) with the awareness they have. Telling someone they are wrong is a violation of their right. It does not mean you have to agree with the other person. It means that what someone is thinking, or feeling is always right for their awareness in that moment.

How willing are you to let go of the past and future? Attachment to the past and future is the only reason you cannot be present. Presence is the basis of forgiveness. What is forgiving? Forgiving is letting go of unloving thoughts about anything or anyone in the past or future. Forgiveness is a direct path into alignment with awareness and Ten.

In this chapter you learned more about your current mindset, and the benefits of reaching a mindset of awareness and acceptance. It seems like a difficult leap, but, in fact, it is simple. Your conditioned mind wants you to think it is difficult. Coming up, you will learn more about how and why this process of un-conditioning your mind can be so beneficial to your quality of life.

6

# PARENTING AND LIVING ARE
# JOURNEYS, NOT DESTINATIONS

I n this chapter you will be introduced to different
definitions of words and concepts than are typically
used and taught. You will learn more about forgiveness, love, and your resistance to them.

## FEAR IS A FOSSIL

*by Spencer Barton*

How can something evolved for human survival be the
greatest impediment to our prosperity and survival as a
species? It wasn't evolved for this, wasn't genetically built for
this. Yeast didn't evolve to live in high-alcohol environments,
but brewer's yeast has adapted to survive better, and humans
can adapt our behavior with far less trial and error than
single celled fungi adapt over millennia.

Fear was protecting animals from danger long before
abstract reasoning was a glimmer in our ancestors' eyes.
Evolution works on "principles" like slow, simple, minor,

independently beneficial changes. There is no science-fiction-style "next stage" in human evolution where we suddenly shed our hair and turn into bald, giant-headed super-geniuses or shed our bodies like husks and live as magical orbs of yellow glowing plasma.

Human beings have long used old evolutionary adaptations in new ways, just as a part of the brain responsible for the gag reflex and physical disgust has been co-opted to feel moral disgust and is implicated, along with the nearby amygdala, in bigotry and violence. The parts and processes of the brain responsible for pleasure and the rearing of young have adapted to experience and promote love, compassion, and cooperation among many other pro-social behaviors.

The next stage in human evolution is whatever those of us who survive and reproduce will pass on to our children who survive and reproduce. Fear is a fossil; one of the many imprints from our vast and continuing infancy as a species. Ideas can change far faster than genes. Last millennium's heretics are this millennium's doctors and scientists. Tribal identity and petty feuds have been extended to national identity and world wars. We must progress to global identity and common goals, lest we wipe one another out at even larger scales than last century.

Fear is the preemption of pain and suffering. The design flaw is that your genome can't tell, and doesn't care (from an evolutionary standpoint), how many false positives (irrational fears) you have, provided you survive and reproduce. Fear emerged from the circuitry for pain; it is, in a primal sense, itself a form of perceived pain. The brain cannot clearly distinguish imagined pain from physical pain, it will react to both in similar ways, such as a cringe or grimace during embarrassment, as well as the pain, fear, and stress responses including fight, flight, or freeze. Being afraid of something biases you to have bad experiences with that thing. Accepting when a fear is irrational is the first step to overcoming it. You must be willing to see it differently, to let it be altered.

Fear and love are both motivators. My ninth grade research essay focused on fear as a motivator in the Rwandan genocide. Rationality is not itself a motivator because the feelings and opinions of good and bad, right and wrong, cannot be derived from the process of reasoning unless you first lay down some fundamental desires and assumptions. Anxiety and ego are both results of runaway fear responses. Meanwhile, acts of love and kindness are expressions of loving desires and assumptions being rationally acted upon to the best of one's ability.

If you have goals that come from love, then achieve them through love. Fear is more than an illusion, it is more than a delusion, it is hardwired, preconscious pain, lack, guilt, shame, and greed. It will at best lead you to a similar outcome via a painful and unpleasant route but being guided by fear can only lead you astray because its only purpose is survival at every cost. The Game of Ten can serve as an instruction manual for using the loving systems of your brain rather than the fearful ones. As you learn to play The Game of Ten later in this book, you will train yourself to see things differently, to be aware without thought, and observant without opinions and judgments. By playing Ten, you also weaken the stranglehold of fear over your mind.

Everyone is doing the best they can with the awareness they have. This includes those coming from love and those people coming from fear, but as fear stifles awareness, it stifles your awareness of the most favorable actions.

I know that fear is a good motivator because it was the only one that ever got me to do my homework when I struggled with executive dysfunction. I was driven by the fear of losing the ability to do the things I love. The fear of being unable to help the people I love, and the fear of loss of love.

The truth is, death is not innately scary, and the loss of love is not real. Fear convinces you that they are real. It is often easier to rationalize emotions as "truth" rather than admit that they are subjective responses based on genes, chemistry, conditioning, and situation. Feelings are true experiences. They are valid, and your emotions are right with the awareness you have. It is simply important to remember that just because something causes fear for one person, does not mean it is scary to every person, or somehow objectively scary.

Fear is a good motivator for doing bad things, or doing "good" things in unhealthy ways. Fear is only a vaguely effective motivator for doing good things, and fear *always* comes with consequences. Love, untainted by fear, is a good motivator for doing good, kind, loving things. Where fear is the mind killer, love is the friend of awareness, acceptance, and logic. Where fear competes with and hates others, love cooperates with and accepts others.

The antidote to the abstraction of fear into the future, is the abstraction of love into all things. Fear begets fear, love begets love, and with a critical mass of kind, loving, accepting people leading by example, a politics of love, as Marianne Williamson calls it, would spread through the population.

Fear is an adaptation for the survival of the individual. Love is an adaptation for the survival of the species and ecosystem. We must therefore learn to interact through love, so that if we cannot help but occasionally react through fear, even anger, it will be understood as a function of biology overwhelming awareness, rather than as a terrible person doing a terrible thing out of pure "evil."

## MILLIE'S STORY

*This story was written several months before my mother, Mary, passed away this past November.* My mother and father, Spencer's grandparents, are ninety and eighty-nine respectively. They have 'round-the-clock' caregivers. They do a wonderful job with my parents, and we are grateful for all that they do.

My parents have a lake house on Sebago Lake about a half hour west of Portland. Millie, one of the caregivers, was without a place to live and could not afford to get a place and pay off her student loans. My parents and sister offered that Millie live with them for the summer at no charge.

Through brief conversations that I had with Millie, she knew of my coaching practice and of the level of intuition I have, but I knew nothing about her personal life, family, or friends. One afternoon in August 2021, I was sitting on the stone patio looking out at the water. Millie came up to me and asked, "How do you forgive?" I was a bit surprised and honored that she asked me this question.

At the time, I was learning and honing my skills at just that subject, forgiveness.

I asked Millie, "Is there a particular person or situation that you want to forgive?"

Her reply was, "Yes, I had a friend. We had been friends our whole life and I had to not be her friend anymore. She was mean to me verbally and emotionally and it got to the point that I had to break away from her. It's been over three years since we've spoken."

I asked her if she was glad that she was no longer in her life. Millie's reply was, "Yes."

I then asked, "You're glad she's not in your life, and you feel guilty that she's not in your life?"

Millie replied, "Yes."

I said, "This is called a dilemma. You don't want her in your life, and you feel guilty that she is not in your life. Now, we're talking about Cathy, right?"

As I mentioned before, I had never talked with Millie about any of her friends. When having attuned and compassionate conversations like this, I am often able to know things about the other person which I have never been told.

As a parent, having deep compassion creates a deeper connection with your child. Deep connections create greater awareness and intuition. It becomes as though all minds are joined, and in the sense that all minds experience awareness, they are.

I asked Millie to think about all the thoughts that she had about Cathy; all the things that hurt her, and all the things she felt about her. Then I said, "When you have all those thoughts and feelings about Cathy gathered, let me know."

She said, "Okay, I have."

Then I said, "Create an altar in your mind. When you've done that, place all those thoughts and feelings about Cathy on that altar and be willing to let go of them, and allow them to be altered."

Millie said, "That's it?"

I replied, "Yup."

My girlfriend Liz and I go over to see my parents every Sunday. Liz always makes a baked treat, and they look forward to seeing us and the treats. One Sunday in the beginning of November, Millie happened to be working and I asked her, "Did you ever hear from your friend Cathy?"

She looked at me and said, "I live with her. Either she changed or I did, and we are friends again and we get along great. We've been living together since September."

Millie's story goes to show the power of forgiveness, and

our ability to both react to and misinterpret others, but also to change and grow from it.

The only timeout I ever gave to Spencer was when I was taking care of him while his mother was away. He was quite young, but verbal. He was upset and misbehaving, and neither he nor I knew it was because he was hungry, something his mother would have likely realized sooner. Eventually we figured it out, I apologized, and he forgave me. We both knew we were doing the best we could with the awareness we had.

For forgiveness to happen naturally and automatically, you must first be willing to forgive, just as you had to be willing to hold a grievance against a person, thing, or situation in the first place. You'll know that you have truly forgiven when the concept of forgiveness no longer makes sense to you. You will feel that there was no reason to hold on to the unloving thoughts about anything. To be in alignment with what is, requires you to be full of love and acceptance and free from all grievances. Grievances are complaints about what is. Think of them as complaints against Ten and against the present state of reality. The complaints you have will keep you in The Game Often Played. If you are not loving a situation, do something about it, or let go of the grievance.

## RESISTANCE

It's time to go deeper into the pool of awareness. The only thing that will stop you is *resistance*. If you have any, great. Be aware of it, allow it, and feel it in your body. In the book, *Beyond The Wall of Resistance*, by Rick Maurer, Maurer identifies three levels of resistance:

Level One: I don't get it.
Level Two: I don't like it.
Level Three: I don't like you.

In Level One, there is the least resistance. Here you might be thinking, "I don't know where this book is going, but I'll give it a chance. What do I have to lose?"

In Level Two, there is greater resistance. You don't like the book. You still might read it, but you're not going to refer it to friends and family. You probably won't use the provided information or tools either.

In Level Three, you're most likely thinking, "These authors are whack-jobs and have no idea what they're talking about." It's nearly impossible to communicate a clear message to someone at this level. If you are at this level of resistance to this book and its authors, it's likely that this book is in a trash bin.

Resistance comes from the ego, itself a mental manifestation of fear. The only thing that your fear can resist is awareness and the love, peace, and happiness that follow. Be aware when you feel resistance. Recognize it for what it is: *fear*. The ego is programmed for this. It fears love, it fears the weakening of itself, in other words, it fears that you will discover who you are.

When you find who you are, the "you" beneath your awareness, will recognize the ego as an imposter and saboteur. The ego (used as defined by *A Course in Miracles*, rather than by Freud), is a false sense of self which many people self-identify with. It's a bit like an artificial intelligence or effigy dreamt up by your mind, with the naïve goal of keeping you, or "itself" safe by any means necessary. We describe negative, painful, and illusory thoughts as coming from ego, from Off-Ten, or from The Game Often Played.

Remember, thoughts affect your experience of reality. It is your responsibility to know where they are coming from. One indication is, if they are loving thoughts, they are coming from awareness, from Ten. If they are unloving thoughts, they are from the ego, and they will always come at a cost.


## LOVE

Let's define *love* as it relates to The Game of Ten. Love is unconditional, absolute, and abundant joy, peace, truth, awareness, and atonement. It is giving without strings attached. Love is acceptance of what is. Love is the one and only program run by awareness. It's a win-win program. In the future chapters, love, and all aspects of love, will often be called Ten.

In all relationships, including parenting, there are written or unwritten rules, boundaries, and expectations. In parent-child relationships, there are many societal expectations which may or may not apply in your specific case, nor should every tradition be followed blindly. As a parent of a minor, you have a responsibility to remain dedicated and responsive in the relationship. If your child is breaking rules or struggling, you are expected to create proportional responses and find solutions.

In relationships other than parenting and guardianship, if any participant is unhappy or violates the terms of the relationship, you don't have to remain in that relationship. It is not loving for any participant to remain in an abusive relationship. If you choose to work on the relationship, great. If you're done, that's also great. You can love and accept everyone as they are; you don't have to be with them.

*Sometimes love says yes.*
*Sometimes love says no.*
*Sometimes love says stay.*
*Sometimes love says go.*

I hope for your sake and theirs that the love you have for your child is unconditional. It is your responsibility to demonstrate this unconditional love to your child, so they may develop this love and acceptance of themselves and others. There are no different expressions of love. There are different boundaries and expectations in different relationships, but every relationship can and should be grounded in love and respect.

All love can be unconditional. Romantic relationships are conditional: "I'll love you if you love me." Attraction is conditional: "I'll love you if you behave and look a certain way." If you meet someone and they say, "You complete me," run for the hills. Or go to couples counseling, please. Whatever level of awareness you are playing from, you are likely to attract a partner who is playing from a similar level, or someone who will attempt to bring you down to theirs.

The fact is, we are all *love*. Every human being on this planet is an expression of love. When we bring this love to our awareness, we give it unconditionally. Some people may be resistant to your love or how you express it. Love that too. Respect is love and respecting your boundaries and the boundaries of others is the only loving thing to do.

*"You have to love everyone. You don't have to have lunch with them."*

— MARIANNE WILLIAMSON

Imagine that you are one big ball of unconditional love, in other words, imagine that you are playing from Ten. You meet another big ball of love. You both decide to have a relationship. Love from Ten can merge and separate with ease. They don't complete you; you are already complete; and you can choose to be with this person or not. This dynamic allows you to embrace and share love without being controlled by it.

> *"The course does not aim at teaching the meaning of love, for that is beyond what can be taught...The opposite of love is fear, but what is all-encompassing can have no opposite..."*
>
> *"Nothing real can be threatened.*
> *Nothing unreal exists.*
> *Herein lies the peace of God."*
>
> — *A COURSE IN MIRACLES*

This is the premise of *A Course in Miracles*. Eckhart Tolle begins one of his lectures with this premise, then goes on to say, "If you understand the meaning of this, you don't have to be here." If you are willing to see things differently, then you will. All your thoughts, feelings and emotions either come from love or fear. One is real and cannot be threatened. The other does not exist. Herein lies your peace.

If you decide to go deeper into awareness and acceptance, you will have a complete change in perception. Much of what you think is, *isn't*; and a lot of what you think isn't, *is*.

You will move from The Game Often Played to The Game of Ten. You will move from the dualistic thinking of cause and effect into the awareness that you are the cause of your life, not the effect of it. It's a complete paradigm shift, from the "normal" way of thinking to the "natural" way of thinking, which is awareness from Ten, a move from misalignment to alignment; a shift from what you thought was counterintuitive, to what is intuitive.

You will move from the world of paradox to the world of orthodox, knowing that which is true. Many ancient religions of India incorporate Karma; though it has many interpretations, a western approximation is *"what goes around comes around."* By being in alignment with awareness from Ten, all "karmic debts" are paid. Don't worry if these concepts sound a bit frightening. You don't need to understand Karma to understand The Game of Ten. Remember that this fear is your resistance to acceptance and awareness. Observe it, allow it, and feel it for as long as it takes to fade and leave you feeling at peace once more. Remember, the only thing we can fear is love. This is a difficult concept. Come up for air and take deep breaths when processing these claims. We have introduced many ideas leading up to The Game of Ten, and any unclear concepts will likely make more sense if you revisit them after reading the upcoming chapters.

You are seeing that love, forgiveness, and resistance may be more than what you thought they were. If this is the case, you're doing great. If you are resisting it in every way, that is also great. You're being given the tools to lean into resistance; to break through the mental blocks which have been holding you back and keeping you stuck in thought patterns and situations that no longer serve you.

# 7

# HOW THE GAME OF TEN WAS CREATED

I n this chapter, you will learn about the influences and origin of The Game of Ten, which will be properly introduced in Chapter 8. We believe The Game of Ten will bring you from an average parent to a super parent. I call it a game because playing around with things leads to learning, and prepares humans and animals for living. Games can have rules which challenge us to think in ways we wouldn't think in everyday life. Changing your assumptions about life can be frightening but trying out a game might be quite fun.

You learn the rules as you play. You can either learn by suffering or you can learn from joy. It depends on which game you choose. You are here to recreate (*re-create*). You may ask yourself, "What am I here to re-create?" You are hard wired to re-create your "heaven" on earth and, by extension, to play, which will help you to achieve this state of recreation and joy.

After my out-of-body/ near-death experience in 1992, I have been on a quest to find the truth of who we are as human beings, and what makes us behave as we do. In 2015 I enrolled at the Gestalt International Study Center to be trained as a business and mindset coach. This gave me a widely accepted method through which to work with clients, using the Gestalt Core Concepts and Behaviors.

To be a great parent, we feel it's important to have a practical understanding of psychology. Although The Game of Ten shares many similarities with many forms of therapy, there are many better-informed psychological resources than our book if you are specifically looking for evidence-based parenting tools. The paper that you are about to read was presented as part of my requirement to graduate from the Gestalt International Study Center (GISC). I'm currently working with Marianne Williamson, Dr. Angela Lauria, the amazing team at Difference Press, The Author Incubator, and Miracle Minded Coaching. Marianne Williamson is a prominent face and voice of *A Course in Miracles* (ACIM). She has been teaching it around the world for more than thirty-five years.

Mary Anne Walk was my coach at the Gestalt International Study Center at the time and is now my dear friend. I have been blessed to have such wonderful mentors, teachers, and friends throughout this journey to awareness and I look forward to meeting and learning from many others along the way.

## AWARENESS: RELATING THE GESTALT CORE CONCEPTS AND BEHAVIORS TO THE TEACHINGS OF *A COURSE IN MIRACLES* AND ECKHART TOLLE

Fritz Perls developed Gestalt psychology in the 1940s and 1950s as a new approach to psychotherapy. It was influenced by eastern philosophy and has been developed and added to by others over time. According to his theory, one of the primary objectives of Gestalt therapy is the ability to restore self-awareness, which is lost, in whole or in part, when a psychological disorder becomes evident. This is accomplished by restoring the individual's ability to differentiate between what is and what is not a true part of the self, which provides the individual with a sense of self-realization, achievement, and awareness.

Awareness is pervasive in all aspects of one's life and theoretically applies to the "Gestalt Core Concepts and Behaviors" used by the Gestalt International Study Center. The GISC "Core Concepts and Behaviors" definitions help to explain how the unconditioned mind, the conditioned mind, and consciousness work together and in opposition to one another.

It is my goal to show you that the Gestalt Core Concepts and Behaviors along with the teachings of Eckhart Tolle and the teachings of *A Course in Miracles* have the same purpose: to bring one to conscious awareness. Some common terms we use for this are: stillness, peace, aliveness, oneness, is-ness, joy, contentment, spirit, and love.

Information supporting this interconnectedness comes from the teachings of *A Course In Miracles* published in 1976. The course uses both logical argumentation and spiritual language to teach the reader how to surrender their "ego" to "spirit" through "forgiveness" thus bringing the reader to awareness.

The lectures of Eckhart Tolle, the author of *The Power of Now* and *A New Earth*, will also be used to substantiate the premise of this interconnectedness to one another and the self. Eckhart Tolle's approach to the subject of awareness is that love, stillness, and peace, which are present in aware-ness, can only be experienced in "the now." The "portal" to awareness, being now.

The goal in coaching is to bring awareness of awareness

to awareness; this is also known as meta-awareness. This is similar to mindfulness and introspection. The ultimate achievement in a coach-client relationship is recognition (re-knowing) of the aware unconditioned mind, combined with recognition that the conditioned mind reflects ingrained and emotional thought patterns, rather than objective reality. This creates a conscious wholeness of mind and being. It is my assertion that with this awareness, the client will be able to use their mind in a more natural, comfortable, and effective way.

For the sake of clarity, it is necessary to explain a spiritual and unscientific perspective regarding how the mind works, similar to the perspective of *A Course in Miracles*, and similar to Plato's "Allegory of the Cave" in its description of subjective experience and interpretation. In his book, The Other Voice, Brent Haskell, PhD claims to be channeling Jeshua, "Jesus."

Dr. Haskell gives more information and explanations of the teachings of *A Course in Miracles*. It is important to keep in mind that the references to Jesus, God, or Spirit are meant to be received with a psycho-spiritual context in mind, with no intended relationship to a particular religion or religious belief system. When no word or words can accurately name this concept of "unconditioned awareness," these words have become a few of the representative ones.

You may be wondering, if what you are about to read has anything to do with being a great parent. Well, the more that you know about how the mind works, the better you will parent. The next few paragraphs are dense. Like *A Course in Miracles*, this too was channeled.

"It is important that we be able to embrace the fact that the production of this world was undertaken within a full state of awareness, and that everything that seems to happen here is by careful design. No mistakes have been made, and no blunders have caused us to seem to be trapped in space and time. Granted it SEEMS otherwise. But that, too, must be part of the design. If that were not so, we would not be invulnerable, and the Course would be in error.

Thus, it is that we desired to make a world, which would have the APPEARANCE of accomplishing the impossibility of separation, all the while being fully aware that it was not actually possible to do so.

This demanded a scheme whereby we could design this world of separation, somehow forget that we had done so, and then look upon that same design and believe it to be a reality. We must realize that this required creative genius at its best. And we have done a masterful job of making such a world.

The manner in which we did this is essentially the same as the way we create our own sickness. The world was not an accident. It is a carefully laid plan of self-deception; whose purpose is to hide reality. We made it up, then devised a clever plan for forgetting that we had done so, and then proceeded to look upon the plan and seem to experience it as being real. The means by which we were able to do this is most clever indeed.

We first imagined that it was possible to actually BE what we cannot be, which is separate from God, and Life itself. In the next instant, in order for that imagined notion to survive, it was necessary for us to seem to split our mind. This simply means that there had to be a part of the mind that was not aware of the carefully laid plan of separation, while another part was fully aware of that same plan and its guaranteed outcome, or the end of the dream of separation, if you will.

In order to do this, we devised projection and perceptions. We made up a screen onto which we could project whatever we wanted to seem to experience in this world of illusion. This is the screen of consciousness. We then projected the chosen images onto that screen, and in an instant split our awareness so that part of our awareness could focus on the screen and pretend that the images were of reality, without remembering where the images came from in the first place.

This was done by the self-same mind that was now looking upon what it had projected. We could not actually BE separate, but we could manage to look upon the set of projected images and pretend that they represented something real. However, the images are not real, and can never be so. Thus, it is that, in reality, this world never happened.

The exciting and possibly alarming insights are the ones that follow. We must ask the nature of the screen onto which mind projected its dream of illusion, and the nature of the images which it chose to project there. And this is the answer. THE SCREEN, WHICH THE MIND CREATED AND ONTO WHICH IT CHOSE TO PROJECT ITS ILLUSIONS OF CONSCIOUSNESS ITSELF, AND THE IMAGES THAT IT PROJECTED ARE NONE OTHER THAN THE THOUGHTS THAT DWELL IN OUR CONSCIOUSNESS. That is why the Course accurately states the screen is the RECEPTIVE mechanism.

It is simply the screen onto which our mind projects that which it would perceive. That is why consciousness was the first split introduced into the mind after the separation was imagined, making the mind the perceiver, rather than the creator. And that is why our thoughts here are nothing but images we have made. The Course tells that 'Perception involves an exchange, or translation, which knowledge does not need.' The exchange, or translation, is the process whereby an image is projected, the process is instantly forgotten, and the self-same mind then views what it projected the moment before. And, finally, that is why the thoughts of which we are aware, the thoughts of consciousness are not our real thoughts, and truly have nothing to do with real thought which do and must reflect the creative power of the unconditioned mind itself."

This excerpt from the prologue of Dr. Haskell's book explains the process of how we separate from truth and enter illusion; how we go from The Game of Ten to The Game Often Played.

Thoughts emanating from awareness are the only thoughts that reflect reality. With that said, I will explain how these concepts relate to the GISC Core Concepts and Behaviors. The italicized paragraphs have been copied and/or paraphrased from the official GISC core concepts and behaviors document.

## GISC CORE CONCEPTS AND BEHAVIORS

### Awareness

*Gestalt believes that the individual or system is performing at its optimum based on its current awareness. At the center of the Gestalt perspective is the concept of awareness. If we believe in the potential of an individual and their self-responsibility, then key to effecting change in the individual is through the expansion of their awareness. By raising awareness, we enable the individual or the organization to*

*maintain responsibility and make the changes that are most appro-
priate and in their best interests.*

This core concept relates to bringing awareness (the
unconditioned mind) to the unaware, "conditioned egoic
mind." The more aware they are, the more possibilities and
choices will be visible and available to the individual or organization.

Awareness can only emerge by observing your thoughts,
emotions, and senses. The client becomes this silent
observing awareness by simply observing their thoughts,
emotions, and senses, noticing these things without judging
or assigning meaning to them. As this presence grows, the
space to expand into consciousness is created.

### Boundary

*The point (contact) at which the "me" and "not me" is made or
broken. It is also the point of intention.*

From awareness comes knowledge. The conditioned mind
is structured to turn the knowledge into "thought forms." It
forgets it knows and then says, "I think" instead of "I know."
It gathers, grabs, and holds on to as many thoughts and as
much information as possible. It stores them and projects
them onto the screen of consciousness. The "me, myself, and
I" has split from the aware self. Awareness says, "I am" while
the ego says, "I am me." Awareness is the intentional "I am."
The "I am me" is misguided and unintentional. It thinks it is
possible to create its own illusory world, separate from the
unconditioned mind, which creates knowledge, yet is not
possessed by thought.

The self-identification with some phenomena as "me" and
other phenomena as "not me" is contradictory to the practice
of unbiased awareness. The conditioned mind's thought

structure creates a boundary, (also called the ego or the mind-made self) and the conditioned mind will resist attempts to change these thought patterns or penetrate these boundaries. It is the role of the coach to bring you back to awareness of these thought patterns and allow you to consciously choose to move the boundary or remove it altogether.

Parents, your thoughts may not accurately represent reality. You may be projecting your own conditioned patterns onto your child. It is important to see through your projections, as though you were an unbiased onlooker to your thoughts and behaviors. This practice of active self-reflection becomes active self-awareness. Once you have developed this awareness, you will be better able to ride out your emotional reactions, and to align your actions with your unconditional love of yourself and your child.

### Contact

*Contact is the term used to define the nature and qualities of human interactions. Individuals are always in contact with their environment and often with other people. The extent to which the individual is aware, present, and engaged, reflects their level of contact.*

The degree to which an individual identifies with the mind-made self, full of tangled thoughts, feelings, emotions, and meanings, will determine how open they will be to reconnecting with their innate awareness. Contact can be closer to awareness of self, when you are emotionally unattached from, and therefore aware of yourself. In other words, it is important to notice and observe your thoughts, feelings, emotions, and senses without needing to self-identify with them. The mind-made self is enhanced by creating stories. of "I, me, and my," which automatically disconnect the thinker from awareness.

So, parents, be aware of the interactions and conversations that you are having with your child. Children can express love and ask for it in unexpected ways. Having greater awareness of your internal and external situation leads to greater contact with your child and greater understanding of their situation.

### Cycle of Experience

*Gestalt is focused on building skills in the process of perceiving, deciding, acting, and learning and improving. The Cycle of Experience describes an interactive cycle that moves from awareness through contact, action, integration, and closure, providing both a framework and a template to observe for competence and areas that need further development.*

Throughout the "Cycle of Experience" is contact and resistance. At each contact there is "resistance." This resistance is an expression of the egoic conditioned mind. Thoughts and patterns that worked in the past are assumed to be useful in the future, not in the present moment.

Although the mind created the ego with the intention of keeping "you" safe, fear and self-doubt become primarily produced by the ego, rather than prevented. In Gestalt, the cycle of experience is depicted as a bell curve and underlying the bell curve is "resistance." My assertion, based on the teachings of A Course in Miracles and Eckhart Tolle, is that plots of "awareness" and "resistance" would add clarity to it, and would be inversely proportional to one another. Resistance peaks at the point of "action" and then subsides with integration and closure. This is a clear indication that the conditioned mind is conditioned to resist awareness.

## Experiments

*Gestalt practice is distinct because it moves toward action, away from "talking about," and for this reason is considered an applied approach. Through trying new ways of doing things, it supports the individual's direct experience of something new, instead of merely talking about the possibility of something new.*

The ego is resistant to change. It is tricky and needs to be transcended in order to break the illusory model of the world which it has created. By experimenting with scenarios through roleplay of previously challenging or resistance-inducing situations, you can work on bringing awareness to your resistance and your child's resistance, thereby helping the child feel less defensive and less likely to hold on to harmful past conditioning. Beneath the ego's past conditioning is the formless which also can be called stillness, love, peace, joy, awareness, and the un-manifest; everything the ego fears and doubts and shields itself from in all its fear-based ways.

## Figure/ Ground

*Some things are more important to you than others, and what you choose to arrest your gaze upon shapes the experience of your life. How you perceive information that is available to you, and how you choose what action you will take, depends on the full amount of information that is available (ground). This includes situation data as well as data about your physical and emotional reaction and experience. From that you make choices about what you will focus on (figure) above anything else. The greater the groundwork, the better the figure. Raising awareness is often about adding information to the ground before a person, group, or organization chooses to focus on a figure.*

Eckhart Tolle refers to a similar concept of life situation:

Who you think you are, while living in the world of form; your job, social status, physical appearance, and your story of I, me, and my. None of it is who you are. They are thought forms of who you are; the thoughts about your life situation keep you from awareness. Awareness is knowing, from a position of silent observation, rather than from a cycle of perceiving, projecting, and judging what you or others think to be true. This awareness can only be pointed to by words and thoughts. Awareness cannot be experienced through these "signposts" which guide you to it. Knowing who you truly are is beneficial to knowing who your child truly is.

The description of figure/ ground relates to many concepts discussed throughout this book. What you focus on impacts your perceptions, actions, and quality of life. Your situation, emotional state, and physical state all contribute to your perceptions and decisions, and therefore, affect what you focus on. By discussing tools and processes for raising awareness, we intend to guide you toward a beneficial feed-back-loop of improved state of mind, improved actions, improved environment, and intentionally chosen figures of focus.

### Gestalt Phenomenology

*Stay with what is-now. Staying with the process.*

Using the Core Concepts and Behaviors, awareness of what "is" unfolds for you. Both Eckhart Tolle and A Course in Miracles go into detail to explain the mind's ability to create the thought form of time. The ego's mind-made self-lives in the past, where it feeds on thoughts of guilt and shame. (Could, would and should, the "-oulds" as we named them in the 2015 GISC coaching program).

Then there is future thinking, which the thinking mind

feeds on voraciously, driven by fear, grasping for thoughts, material possessions and knowledge; things and possibilities of things, that should, would, or could happen in the future. The only outcome is worry, anxiety, and fear of never having or being "enough."

The truth is, there is only the "now." Now is still itself a "thought form," yet a "thought form" that points to awareness; as a portal or signpost to awareness, if you will.

As a parent, it is important to stay present with your child. Staying aware of the present moment and aware of how the ego uses the concepts of past and future to keep you out of the present, can be quite useful in parenting and daily living.

### Intention

*When you operate without awareness, you operate without intention. Unexpected and disappointing consequences often emerge when decisions and actions are taken without intention. As you become more aware, you are better able to make decisions and take actions from a point of clear intention. This often results in meeting your needs and the needs of your child more fully. Clarifying intentions is especially important when raising awareness.*

Clarity can only be achieved by letting go of the past and overcoming the desire to constantly grasp at the future. Letting go and forgiving are one and the same. Fear and wanting are the motivators of the egoic mind. Intentions will be clouded by these worries and desires unless they are observed for what they truly are.

## Level of System

*Things are happening everywhere, all the time. You experience anxiety, you and your child have an argument, a group decides to act, an organization experiences a trauma. When you are working with a system, you need to increase your awareness of what is happening and at what level and determine how you want to impact the system at what level. Understanding how people, groups and organizations work allows you to see how best to influence and impact their success.*

Through awareness, you can see a situation as it is in the present moment. Knowing what to change or keep the same is important to achieving your desired outcome and avoiding unintended consequences. Every system functions as it is set up to function. Not every system functions as it is intended to function. This understanding explains many things, including how the good intentions of the fearful, egoic mind lead to hellish misery.

## Multiple Realities

*We emphasize the concept of multiple realities and acknowledge that we each bring our unique experience and perception to a situation, and that there are always multiple ways of making meaning out of a given moment – all of which are real to the individual. We place great emphasis on teaching people how to manage differences.*

Perceptions are points of view. A Course in Miracles, Eckhart Tolle, and the GISC all view perceptions as illusions; models of the real world which may be useful but are not the world itself. A point of view is a piece of "the whole view" which the ego believes to be the only view because it is unable to comprehend true wholeness.

Awareness of and acceptance of different points of view is the only way to heal the separation and to be aware of your innate wholeness. Points of view are neither right nor wrong. They are simply frameworks of interpretation which one may hold. Given past experiences and thoughts, you, your child, or a group, all make the best decisions and choices that they can make with the awareness they have at a given moment.

What is the meaning of life? You may as well ask the meaning of trees. Things in this world don't have to have a meaning, often they just are. They exist because they can exist. They have a how, so they don't need a fundamental why. The question then becomes, what meaning do you have in life? What meaning improves your life? What do you find pleasure and purpose in doing?

Acceptance doesn't just counter-out denial, it means moving beyond the need for denial and moving into a different understanding entirely. Normal does not mean happy. Normal doesn't mean good or bad, it's just the average portion within the evolutionary and social numbers game (the middle of the curve, the middle of the normal distribution). Everyone is natural, even if we are not all normal.

### Optimistic Stance

*Gestalt takes a realistic view of the present and an optimistic view of the possible, preferring to work in the development of the potential within an individual or system rather than correcting them.*

The "present" is the only realistic view of time. There is only now, there will only be now. It is the eternal time. Letting go of past thought forms and future thought forms is the only way to be present. "Letting go" is another way of saying "forgiving." An optimistic stance is saying "yes" to the moment as well as to the individual or system. It creates a space of awareness where creativity is possible and available.

When your child is misbehaving or doing something you do not approve of, taking an optimistic stance means recognizing that this can be a teachable moment rather than a cause for punishment.

### Polarities

*Polarities are the natural process of opposites. There is a tendency to move to one side and call it a good thing and to call the other side bad. Our stance is that both ends of every polarity are important, depending on the circumstance. Growth and development are the stretching to incorporate the whole spectrum.*

Polarities become evident when the mind-made-self separates from awareness. The product of this unaware self-identification is the ego. The ego is created out of fear. Fear both clouds the awareness and promotes self-identification with our thoughts, traits, and possessions out of a fear of loss of self, loss of life, and ultimately, loss of love.

The ego's simplistic judgments and categorizations of dichotomies like good or bad, right, or wrong, and victim or oppressor, create a fear-based view of a world at war with you and with itself. This easily leads to xenophobia, bigotry, and thoughts like "Everyone's out to get me" or "It's us versus them!" The ego sees the poles at either end of a continuum but ignores the field or spectrum in between. The ego believes that cause has an opposite effect. It fails to recognize that causes are also effects, and effects are also causes. Polarities are one such illusion which is assigned importance when the mind sees the world from a viewpoint of fear rather than a viewpoint of awareness, acceptance, and love.

By becoming aware that the poles of any thought form are both parts of the same continuum with varying degrees, you allow yourself to see each situation with greater awareness.

The goal of this book is to bring you beyond the poles good/ bad and to a space of acceptance of "what is." This place has no opposites. True peace of mind is not on a spectrum, it just is.

### Presence

*Who you are as an individual and how you present yourself when you are with others is at the core of your presence. In Gestalt, it is believed that your presence has the ability to impact another person, group, or organization. Becoming increasingly aware of your presence and acting with intention on how you can use your presence is a discipline of Gestalt. Whether you are modeling a behavior, bringing a missing presence, or joining an existing energy, you are always having an impact.*

Being present with your child is an important part of parenting. As you know, being present can be difficult in this era of social media and cell phones, but it is a challenge worth overcoming. Presence according to Eckhart Tolle is the space beneath your thoughts, emotions, and sense perceptions. It is the space of the unconditioned mind, a space of awareness, stillness, aliveness, love, and joy. Presence is essential in parenting. If you are thinking from a place other than presence, then your child is not receiving a full parent-child experience.

### Resistance

*It is a force that slows or stops movement. It is a natural and expected part of change. Understanding the resistance and leaning into it releases energy to move forward. It is a paradox.*

Resistance is when the mind says "no" to what is. The ego is always in a state of resistance. It resists here, now, and enough, by keeping your mind dwelling in the past or grasping at the future through thought. The ego believes that it is protecting you because it believes that it is you. The ego functions as it is set up to function, not as it was intended to function. The ego was built by thoughts and worries. It sits on a foundation of fear, and it desires complete control in order to destroy everything which it fears. Fear evolved to aid in survival and avoidance of pain and death. The ego's goal was to minimize pain and maximize pleasure, but nothing built from fear and control can bring true pleasure. Your ego hates you because it cannot control you, but it tells you that it's protecting you and that it loves you. An egoic thought would be, "If I can just do more, plan better, and control more, then finally I'll be happy." Your ego's resistance to the reality of your needs and capabilities is a basic explanation of self-loathing and self-destruction. The ego is an unreal construct synthesized within your mind which wants you to believe you are separate from peace, separate from love, and separate from others. It resists love. This is what we mean by "The only thing you can resist is love," or, "The only thing you can fear is love." The ego and its resistance to reality become conditioned over time, but the good news is that your brain can be reconditioned through acceptance and love.

A Course in Miracles refers to this as "natural versus normal." The constant flow of awareness and acceptance is our "natural" state of mind. The resistance to this movement is our "normal" state of mind. In other words, the ego resists and the unconditioned mind "spirit" does not. By getting to know what inspires you and your child, your movement from "normal" to "natural" becomes much easier.

## Self-Responsibility

*Gestalt firmly believes in the responsibility and dominion of the individual or system for itself. It is only by taking responsibility for your decisions and actions that you are able to change and improve your experience and interaction in the world. It is up to the individual or system to change itself.*

Inner change comes from within by definition, but external changes can hurt us, kill us, replace us, and catch us by surprise. Only take responsibility for that which you are responsible. Just because you can influence your thoughts, interpretations, and perceptions doesn't mean you can always control the people and world around you, and it doesn't mean that you have to sit back and accept misery or injustice while blaming yourself for not having enough "gratitude." While complaining can lead you to stewing in misery, talking to others about your situations, feelings, and concerns can be extremely helpful in providing another viewpoint or simply a moment to observe, feel, allow, and eventually let go of these things. You have the ability to raise your awareness and the awareness of others regarding both personal and collective situations. To point out the cause of a phenomenon is different than diverting responsibility from yourself. It may be up to the individual or system to change itself, but it is also up to individuals within a system to change that system.

To the conditioned egoic mind, responsibility is for others. It does not apply to the ego, where there is plenty of blame, guilt, and shame to make it perfectly clear to itself and others that change is not possible because "the others" are making it so. It is a victim of its false self. Alternatively, when not blaming others for its own actions, your conditioned mind can also blame yourself for situations brought about by others, and by circumstances beyond your control. It is important to note that self-judgment and self-hatred are only possible because the mind-made self believes it is both you and better than you. Like an arrogant authoritarian, your thoughts believe they can change and control you, and they make it appear to be your fault when they cannot. Your ego will take responsibility for your successes and lead you to blame yourself for all perceived failures, rather than recognizing that you are doing the best you can with the awareness you have; an awareness notably hampered by constantly attending to a judgmental voice inside one's head.

Through understanding this concept, the coach and client allow the process of change to occur from a clear position. This becomes a position of responsibility and self-awareness. Teaching this concept to your child at a young age is vital to helping them to grow into a healthy, happy, and responsible person, one who takes responsibility, and does not assign undue blame onto themselves or others.

### Shadow Self

*The shadow self is a psychological term introduced by the late Dr. Carl Jung. It is everything in us that is unconscious, repressed, undeveloped and denied. There are rejected aspects of your being, so there is positive undeveloped potential in the shadow because (by definition) anything that is unconscious is not in your awareness. Healing comes from the shadow. When you integrate your shadow side, you become aware of your belief in your own inferiority, your vulnerability, weakness, and greed. Gestalt has adopted Jung's theory because it is central to self-awareness and the integration of whole being.*

*A Course in Miracles* and Eckhart Tolle would both call the Shadow Self the "ego," (particularly, the shadow is similar to the assumptions hidden within the ego, rather than the egoic thoughts which become conscious). Tolle has also called it various iterations of the "conditioned, mind-made self." The shadow remains a shadow until it is brought into the light of awareness.

The ego/ shadow does not want to be discovered and will do everything in its power to remain as the shadow. Simply by noticing or observing these phenomena without judgment or thoughts of yourself and others, the process of awareness will begin bringing the shadow into the light, enabling the emergence of a wholeness of self.

If you want to see your shadow, perceive others. That which you perceive, you project through the screen of consciousness. Only by seeing others, yourself, and situations from an optimistic stance where love, acceptance, and awareness are the only perceptions that are projected, will you see the truth. Living without this awareness will ensure that you will unintentionally project aspects of your shadow onto your child. When the shadow is brought to light it becomes awareness.

### Strategic and Intimate Systems

*Behaviors that create trust and safety and balancing interactions to produce a seamless braid result in the best possible outcome.*

When you are coming from a position of awareness, it is possible to have this seamless experience. Collaboration, unity, and oneness will accomplish the seamless braid. When coming from the thought identified mind, the braiding will get quickly knotted and tangled. Thought identification is the personalization of an idea.

The egoic, mind-made self will use this thought form, attach an emotion to it, and be off on its merry way creating the story of I, me, and my. Its survival depends on this, as does everything in its illusory power, to cling to and perpetuate the story of "you." In parenting, knowing how your child's thought patterns have led them to behave, more strategically or intimately, will help in communication and interaction.

### Theory of Change

*Only an individual, group, or organization can change itself. The challenge of the Gestalt practitioner (coach/ consultant/ clinician) is to raise the awareness of the individual, group, or organization so that it decides to change itself. The paradox is that the more a system attempts to be who it is not, the more it remains the same. Conversely, when people identify with their current experience, the conditions of wholeness and growth support change.*

Your current experience can only happen in the now. Awareness is formless and changeless. It is in a perpetual state of sameness, wholeness, oneness, and "isness." "Forms" are what change. "Thought forms" change. "Life situations" change.

It is important to understand the impermanence of form, of matter, energy, and the patterns they take. Impermanence is a natural condition of any object, thought, or other pattern. If you expect the same forms throughout life, you will be disappointed. As you age, your body changes; you get old, things break, and the forms decay, die, and change.

What remains is the eternal unchanging awareness that you long to connect with during your physical life. The only reason to change is to consciously get closer to being with this awareness. People often mislabel "happy." We are only truly happy when we feel the joy of approaching and reaching full awareness and love.

## Unit of Work

*Each person, group or organization has any number of obligations, responsibilities, expectations, activities, tasks and other "to-dos." Each of these is at various stages of starting and completion. In Gestalt, the process of getting work done requires clarity around what it is that is being done and the stage of the cycle of experience in which we are working. Being explicit about the boundary and stage of work that is to be completed is referred to as a "unit of work." Being clear on a unit of work and completing the unit with effective closure is an important aspect of the Gestalt approach.*

A Course in Miracles dedicates one thousand pages to one concept: "love and forgiveness." In the Course, the only unit of work is letting go of the "thought" of who you are, to then become the awareness of who we are. This is a transformation of the "human doing" (who is trapped in thought), to the human being (who lives from awareness). Your thinking has its purpose in practical living, including making appointments, making decisions, and solving technical problems. The dysfunction occurs when you stay in "thinking mode." When stuck in "thinking mode," rather than allowing you to think your own thoughts, your thoughts begin to "think you" and create your mind-made self.

To avoid this form of self-delusion, you must ensure that your thoughts emerge from, and are observed from a place of awareness. Thoughts are to be played with, and then let go of. They are "for giving," and that is all.

The Course goes on to say that the "only" prayer that can be answered is the prayer of forgiveness of others and yourself. Once accomplished, the concept of "forgiveness" makes no sense because of the realization that it is a mistake in thinking which caused the need to forgive in the first place.

Once thought forms, emotions, and sense perceptions in

the mind are let go or "forgiven," the space of awareness is revealed. In other words, let go or get dragged.

When you bring this process of letting go to the awareness of your child, it allows them to move through their cycle of experience with less resistance.

### Well Developed/ Less Developed©

*GISC teaches "well developed" and "less developed" to describe how people tend to lean to one end of the polarity and call it good and call the other end of the polarity bad. At times you may use the well-developed because it is an automatic way of being. Overuse of any behavior narrows your choices. Understanding well developed/ less developed theory allows for the opening of more possibilities.*

Dualities of thoughts and behaviors are in the realm of form. Truly understanding and accepting when you are operating from this "dualistic form" is important. By noticing and directing your attention toward this "thought form," the duality can merge into a totality. This allows the "flow" of acceptance to open you and your child to the space of formless awareness.

## CONCLUSION

Using *awareness*, and knowledge which guides one to awareness, in parenting is essential to your emotional growth and that of your child. Practicing awareness, with the Gestalt Core Concepts and Behaviors as a template, is one way to accomplish this.

By being present in *the now* (Phenomenology) with your child, you create a space of safety, promoting movement of awareness and understanding through the "cycle of experience." By asking open-ended questions, parental "contact" is made which strengthens the "ground," and a "figure" emerges, leading to better parent-child communication.

By having clear intentions and presence with your child, the conditioned past and anticipated future can be looked at and let go of. Unhealthy emotional barriers come down as resistance diminishes and your increased awareness unfolds.

By coming from an "optimistic stance," "awareness" and "self-responsibility" can be acknowledged by both you and your child. Then, "multiple realities," "polarities" and the "well developed and less developed" can be explored so that your child can gain acceptance of self and others.

Awareness is the key to a successful parent-child relationship.

You may have found this chapter to be a bit dense. Indeed, the GISC terms aren't as concise as the rules of The Game of Ten or The Game Often Played. If you are like most, your conditioned mind will question, doubt, and fight this process at every turn. These middle chapters are a process that you can return to and refer to as many times as you find helpful. This book is designed to be a tool on your parenting journey, as well as a tool to maintain your awareness and mindset of Ten.

8

---

# SETTING UP THE GAME OF TEN

I n Ten you have to see the innocence in everyone and everything. People project guilt onto their environment, onto others, and onto their mind-made-selves from Off-Ten. Everything is innocent in the eyes of Ten.

Ten transcends the spectrum of good and bad; happy and sad. Often people will joke and say that they are eleven or fourteen or so on, these people are either Tens with a sense of humor, or they are playing one through nine and not realizing that their feelings of inadequacy and judgment can be moved beyond; and are thus in denial.

Instead of "I'm a loser" or even "I'm a landscaper" (identifying with your job or expertise) simply think, "I am." "*I am.*" It is one of the simplest sentences, and one which cannot be used against oneself or used to strengthen the ego. What would you say to a good friend? Begin to speak to yourself as a friend, or, better, move beyond the need for such thoughts, and beyond the internal monologue or dialogue of self-talk altogether.

In this chapter you will become more familiar with the rules (Tenets) of the game. It is important to keep it simple.

The game is simple until you overcomplicate it. You can always go back and reread chapters four through nine for reference after completing the book, and we encourage you to do so.

Changing your mindset is a nuanced process in and of itself. As you may know, your brain has impressive neuroplasticity, especially in childhood. As an adult, however, changing and reshaping your mindset can take time, effort, and repetition to build these new habits and pathways in place of the old. Others may try to influence you, but you are the only one who can change your mind. If anything you read and learn in this book works for you, use it. If what you read doesn't, don't. This book is meant to help you create the life that is right for you.

## JANE'S STORY

The Game of Ten was created as an experiment during a one-hour coaching session with a non-paying client to full fill my student hours to graduate. After attending the Gestalt International Study Center in Wellfleet, Massachusetts in 2015, I began my coaching and consulting business. Using the GISC format that was taught during the course, I began a session with a client who I will call Jane. Jane met with me to help her in her business. She taught "etiquette." I was hired to coach her on mindset and awareness to help her grow her business.

We discussed marketing, time management, and many other challenges that arise when running a business. Since the beginning of the first session, a pattern emerged: Jane's family, friends, and her passion for teaching swimming, all came "first." The business, and Jane's personal needs, came in at a not-so-close second. In this session, we discussed her inability to dedicate any time at all for her business because of the demands of her children, her husband, and even the disorganized exchange student she found herself tidying up after.

It became clear to her that she was putting the wants and needs of others far ahead of what she wanted and needed for herself. There was no time or space to run her etiquette business, never mind being successful in it. We ended the session with her feeling ready to commit the time and space for her and the business. To start with, three hours in the following week; a small-time commitment, yet a big leap for Jane.

We met again on the following week. Our sessions were held at a private club of which I was a member. It was a comfortable environment. Two couches that faced each other, a coffee table sat between us, and a fireplace stood to my right, Jane's left.

The session began the same way the first one had. Everyone's needs and wants came before hers. She talked about her husband's job and how he expected supper on the table at a certain time. The children's demands on her continued and she was still consistently cleaning up the exchange student's room, despite nobody asking her to.

I wondered if she had walked away with anything from the last session. The frustration on her face was obvious. Hopelessness emerged as the common theme. Out of the blue, I asked Jane, "Where are you on a scale of one to ten with self-esteem. Jane replied, "a two." She had a smile on her face when she said those words. I asked her, "Where were you on a scale of one to ten at the beginning of our first session. Her reply was, "zero." I was delighted to hear that she had risen two points from our last session. I pointed out that the rise from zero to two is very impressive, and that she was now 20 percent of the way to full self-esteem. A smile emerged as she became aware of the improved life that she was creating for herself.

Then came another out-of-the-blue idea. I asked Jane if she wanted to play a game. She looked puzzled and said, "sure." I had no idea where this was going or what was going to come of this experiment. All I knew was that it felt powerful, and I was going to go with it. I cleared the coffee table and told her we were going to create a board game about her life, to look at how she played a part in it. I asked her if she wanted to give the game a name.

She was unable to come up with a name and asked that I name the game about her life. We put all the people, places, and things she was dealing with daily into the imaginary board game. We talked about the players in the game and the life situations in the game. We put it all on the table, so to speak. We looked long and hard at this game. I noticed that Jane's eyes were welled up. It was a powerful moment of silence. I then suggested that we call this game, "My Life Sucks." Jane burst into laughter and said, "It does!"

The next thing that we did, was to light an imaginary fire in the adjacent fireplace. That being done and acknowledged, I ask her if she would like to pick up the board game with all its pieces and throw it into the fire. Jane gladly burned the game and watched it all go up in flames.

Next, I asked Jane if she wanted to create a new game, with all the people, places, and things that she wanted and needed in her life for it to feel complete in every way. Jane's reply was, "You can do that?" "Yes," I replied.

By this time, I realized that this was going somewhere. I was on a roll and leaning into it. Jane asked me what the new game was called. I said, "It's called The Game of Ten. Here are the rules: You are Ten," Jane's face lit up and a sense of relief came over her. She asked me for more rules. I replied,

"In this game, you are always right with the awareness that you have." "I'm loving this game. Is there more?" Jane said, with a sense of hope and optimism. "Yes," I replied, "You are Ten. You are enough. You do enough. You have enough. Those are the rules."

Jane loved the game. She was beaming from ear to ear. Then came the reality check. I said, "These are the rules that always apply to you. They also always apply to the way you view every person, thing, or situation. That's the hard part." It took Jane a moment to take in the second part of the rule equation. Then with a strength that I had not seen from her, she sat straight up and looked me in the eyes and proclaimed, "I am Ten!"

You're getting there. You're doing great! You likely have a lot of beliefs and programming from the past to unlearn, uncondition, and deprogram. Hopefully you're already seeing the benefits of this different way of thinking and being. You are becoming a parent who is present, loving, and clear of the baggage that has been holding you back all these years. We're setting the stage so you can learn the rules and begin playing The Game of Ten. Ten is the highest score in The Game of Ten. It is the acceptance of what is in the present moment. The mindset of Ten transcends right and wrong, big, and small, nothing and everything. It encompasses all forms of duality. In doing so, it dissolves the illusions of duality, separation, and fear.

## WHAT IS TEN?

*The simplicity of Ten is the beauty of Ten.*

### What Are You Thinking?

The Game of Ten is about overcoming the thoughts, feelings, and beliefs which hold you back from peace and joy. In Ten, you have to see the innocence in everyone and everything. People project guilt onto their environment, onto their mind-made-self, and onto others, from Off-Ten. Everything is innocent in the eyes of Ten.

Your thoughts are mental patterns. They are judgements and beliefs based on your feelings, as well as your perceptions of things and situations. Thinking about a thought, or trying not to think a particular thought, only locks this thought more firmly into the conditioned mind. It will eventually come back to disappoint you from Ten. Your conditioned mind stores thoughts, to be used later to validate a belief that you have about a person, thing, or situation.

Your thoughts may be positive or negative. Thinking that you are smarter than someone, or doing a better job than someone, may seem like positive thoughts at first, but these comparisons require negatively judging another person. This self-aggrandizing comparison will come back later as self-deprecating judgment when you compare yourself to someone you see as "better" or when you don't live up to your own expectations, causing you to feel even worse.

Ten is formless and in a state of complete awareness. When you view your thoughts from Ten, your thoughts are neither good nor bad, they are simply thoughts. A thought that is derived from present moment awareness will keep you in Ten. Only when you hold onto these thoughts, do they bring you Off-Ten. It is like putting the cart before the horse. The thought is the cart, and your awareness is the horse. If thoughts lead and awareness follows, then ego, illusion, worry, and regret can consume the mind. Your awareness exists before, beneath, and beyond thought; it is the observer and experiencer. Allowing thoughts to control awareness is not just illogical, but destructive.

The egoic, conditioned mind thinks that if you let go of all the thoughts that it has remembered for you to keep you safe; you will die. It is afraid that it will die, and it believes that it is you, and you believe that you are it. By letting go of those thoughts you will live. You will live free of guilt and shame, self-doubt, and fear. You will be living a fulfilled life, aligned with all the attributes of Ten.

To borrow and expand upon some terms from *A Course in Miracles*, your thoughts are for giving. Miracles occur when you have your thoughts altered to bring them into alignment with Ten. Any thoughts that occur that are not in alignment with the attributes of Ten, are to be brought to the altar and altered. Unloving thoughts are not derived from Ten's present awareness, rather, they come the egoic, conditioned mind. Ten will never alter a thought without your permission and willingness to have it brought into alignment with awareness.

*A Course in Miracles* states that there is no order of difficulty when creating a miracle. *"One is not 'harder' or 'bigger' than another."* It defines miracles in many ways, including as the expression of forgiveness and love. In the context of The Game of Ten, a miracle can be seen as a shift in your perception, from a misaligned thought to a thought or insight aligned with what we would call the attributes of Ten.

Complaints or grievances keep you out of alignment. They

come from The Game Often Played. They must be brought to a higher level of awareness to be altered. You must be willing to let these grievances go to see yourself, others, and life events differently. You will now be introduced The Game of Ten and its *Tenets* (rules). To play The Game of Ten, you must accept that the Tenets are true for you, and are true for everyone else, whether or not they believe it. Everyone is either Ten or a Ten who is yet to realize it. The best thing we can do for ourselves, and others is to treat everyone as though they are Ten, because they are.

Childhood is the formative period for all humans. Brains grow, wire up, fire up, and eventually prune down in early adulthood to maximize their effectiveness for the world they grew up in. Therefore, the beliefs and feelings one has about oneself, and the formative experiences they have during this period, have an outsized impact on the rest of their life, for better or worse. For the Game of Ten to help the most people in the biggest possible way, it must be shared with people of all ages, and it will be both more easily learned and internalized by children. To internalize The Game Often Played, is perhaps the final step in creating what Eckhart Tolle calls the conditioned mind. On the other hand, to internalize The Game of Ten is the first step to inner peace. The remaining steps are putting it into practice.

## THE GAME OF TEN®

### Tenets
*I am Ten.*
*I am always right with the awareness I have.*
*I am always doing the best I can with the awareness I have.*
*I am enough.*
*I do enough.*
*I have enough.*

To realize that you are Ten, that we are all Ten, and that we never truly left Ten, is the first step in realizing that all pain, suffering, and fear were little more than constructs of the mind, many of which can be alleviated through acceptance. All inferiority and superiority, all debt and wealth, are invented concepts emerging from fear or convenience or greed. Ten is the ultimate means and end of "getting over yourself."

When you realize that everyone and everything is connected, different emergent patterns of the universe playing out different emergent patterns of their respective systems, you can finally let go of existential fear, let go of self-identification with physical and emotional pain, and let go of self-identification with labels, and objects, and behaviors, and people.

True awareness arises when your nervous system is unclouded by guilt, shame, fear, and pain. True awareness is not controlled by thoughts, but uses thoughts as tools for action, and never clings to or identifies with these thoughts. A person living from true awareness, from Ten, may not appear or act noticeably differently in most situations. Awareness does not, after all, rewire one's nervous system or change their mannerisms overnight. Likewise, awareness does not correct physical ailments and imbalances beyond the reach of the mind. We, the authors, both take medication to help manage our symptoms of ADHD by altering our levels of dopamine and norepinephrine. We take antibiotics for bacterial infections and anesthesia during surgery. We suffer physically and emotionally when something brings us Off-Ten, but the same situations have different outcomes when we remember that we are enough, do enough, have enough, are right and doing the best we can with the awareness we have; in short, when we once again realize that we are all Ten.

When you declare that you are Ten, it puts your self-concept on equal footing with the rest of the world. You simply are who you are and were "intended" to be. It is our innate position that we are all appointed as beings. Ten is the highest form of unconditional acceptance of *what is* in this moment. It is the state of peaceful, present awareness. Parenting from Ten is made much easier when you follow these rules and use these tools.

The simplicity of Ten is the beauty of Ten. Ten is the perfection of this moment, when the physical and mental merge to be as one. In this oneness, we are connected to one another at the highest level of awareness. You are complete, whole, and absolute. Ten can be seen as the "unified field" of awareness, the perfect balance of all mental forces. Ten is pure unconditioned consciousness.

Ten is peace. It is love without conditions, void of guilt and shame. It is the space between thoughts. Ten is abundant, giving, and full. Ten is the universal truth of who you are in all ways. It is who, what, how, and why you are here at this moment. It has transcended the "positive and negative" polarities of thought and what you think to be true. Ten is love without fear. You are Ten.

## EVERYONE (AND EVERYTHING) IS ALSO TEN

When you declare yourself Ten, you are declaring everyone and everything to be Ten as well. This understanding aligns you with Ten. Because Ten arises from acceptance, it is always in balance with the world. It is also important to remember that your awareness is always perfectly aligned with Ten, whether or not you realize it. So is everyone else's. If you see a person or situation as less than Ten, you will feel the pain of that judgment, meaning you have dropped Off-Ten, down to the level you perceive the other to be. One through Ten are representations of levels of awareness.

Ten is the highest level of awareness. Observing yourself and realizing when you are unaware (Off-Ten) is key to reaching greater awareness. Of course, you see things that are not right: poverty, sickness, and social injustice. In The Game of Ten, you are not asked to live in denial of these things. You are asked to accept them as they are right now. By accepting things that you want to be different, your state of mind is prepared to make changes from a place of awareness rather than reacting with blind desire and aggression. Often when making changes from reaction, you make the situation worse by creating more of what you don't want. In The Game of Ten, you create a *new now*.

# I AM ALWAYS RIGHT WITH THE AWARENESS I HAVE

### *I Am Doing the Best I Can with the Awareness I Have*

You are always right and doing the best you can with the awareness that you have. Who can argue with this statement? Individuals and group members make the best decisions they can. Your awareness informs you to act in a manner which you *think* is right for yourself, and others, in this moment.

By allowing yourself to be right in this moment, you remain in Ten. "I am always right with the awareness I have, and doing the best I can with the awareness I have," is a declaration of your *innocence*. It feels "right" because it is right. From Ten, you can declare yourself intrinsically right with the awareness you have, without judging anyone to be intrinsically wrong, bad, or less-than Ten.

This statement is absolute, free of all guilt and shame. The results of acting on what you feel to be "right" in this moment may be different from what you had intended. Such a situation is an opportunity to create a new increased awareness of what is right for you and what may be right for others. The only right that is constant is that you are Ten and that you are *right* here, *right* now, always and in all ways. This absolute truth, of being correct with one's awareness, is a key component of accepting responsibility for yourself and allowing others to take responsibly for themselves.

## EVERYONE IS ALWAYS RIGHT WITH THE AWARENESS THEY HAVE

### *Everyone Is Doing the Best They Can with the Awareness They Have*

If the earlier statements are true for you, how can they be otherwise for someone else? Others make choices as best they can, which are right for them at any given moment. Accepting that others are making the best choices they can based on their awareness and situation, allows you to see things differently. It opens up possibilities for collaboration and compassion which may have been impossible if you saw the other person as innately wrong.

The understanding that "everyone is doing the best they can with the awareness they have" may be the single most important lesson we can convey to you. It snaps people out of their victim or protagonist worldviews and reminds them that everyone is doing the very best they can at that moment. "The best they can," refers to their current physical and mental capabilities, as well as the physical and perceived constraints of the situation they are in. "The awareness they have," refers to both their knowledge and their brain's current capabilities. The kindest, most knowledgeable, most consistent person in the world would probably appear to be none of those things after four days of sleep deprivation, a near-miss with a pack of wolves, and a recent concussion. Indeed, the kindest, most knowledgeable, most consistent person is already extremely lucky that their past and present aligned to promote those features, rather than hindering the development thereof.

Saying, "Everyone is doing the best they can with the

awareness they have," is not an argument for complacency in a murderous or exploitative system, nor is it a defense of the actions of hurtful or murderous individuals. On the contrary, it is the most fundamental explanation of those unaware actions.

Accepting that everyone is doing the best they can with the awareness they have, is the first step to understanding that the good and bad aspects of the world, rather than caused exclusively by a few saints and a few bad apples, are emergent from the systems within and around every one of us. Unhealthy, unhappy, uninformed people are less likely to make decisions which benefit the health, happiness, and awareness of themselves and others. Even the judgments of "good" and "bad" actions are subjective, relying on what a person or group interprets to be moral, justifiable, or useful.

We will be the first to admit that when you properly define "the best they can" and "the awareness they have" it is not a falsifiable statement. Show us someone who is not doing the best they *could* be doing, and we will show you someone who is doing the best they *can* with the awareness they have. It is not falsifiable, and it also makes perfect sense. This unfalsifiable assertion is a powerful weapon against the illusions and tricks of the ego. Once the knowledge that *everyone is doing the best, they can with the awareness they have* becomes part of your fundamental assumptions, you will have no use for judgmental thoughts. You will realize that guilt, shame, hatred, and blame have no basis in reality, and no place in a life lived from Ten. "The awareness they have," also describes one of the easiest, yet most far reaching catalysts for change and improvement: *the raising of awareness*. Raising awareness can refer to both promoting inner peace, as well as learning and sharing facts and ideas about the world, which people were otherwise unaware of.

## I AM ENOUGH. I DO ENOUGH. I HAVE ENOUGH.

Let's discuss "enough." *Webster's College Dictionary* defines "enough" as "adequate for the want or need; sufficient for the purpose or to satisfy desire."

Ten is enough. It is never more or less than what is needed in the moment. It can never be otherwise, neither can you. All that you are is enough for right now. In The Game Often Played, your opinions of what is enough will frequently change. Within this vortex of ever-changing needs and wants, enough is the only constant. When you accept your innate state of *being, doing,* and *having* enough, you will have no need for greed or self-hatred. This concept is also the basis for manifestation. The concept of "ask and you shall receive," must come from a position of enough, rather than a position of need and want (as seen in Chapter 4: The Game Often Played: One to Six).

"I am enough" is the ultimate value statement which breaks down the "scarcity" mindset of incompleteness and lack. When you know that you are enough, you can overcome the urges to acquire ever more possessions or to do ever more value-affirming activities. When you know you are enough, you can finally overcome the vicious never-ending cycle of needing, wanting, and lacking; of seeking the unreachable horizon of enough.

"I do enough" is an extension of this value statement because we so often judge ourselves by our interpretation of our actions, and society has reinforced this tendency to define oneself by what one does, and how much one does. "What do you do?" is a very normal question for one American to ask another at a party or gathering, I frankly prefer "How do you do?" Also consider the response "busy" to the question "how are you?" it says almost nothing. Is the person exhausted? Physically active? Euphoric? None are ruled out by the term "busy" which we often take to mean "over-worked" or "productive" even though terms like "busywork" refer to the exact opposite of productivity.

"I have enough" is the affirmation which most toes the line between subjective experience and objective reality. To believe someone "has the right stuff" or "has a kind heart" are clearly similar moral value statements to being enough and doing enough. On the other hand, a starving man who, in his delirium says, "I have enough," and promptly dies, clearly did not have enough food to survive, only enough food to die. Starvation is a material condition, not a mindset. The Game of Ten is a path to enlightenment, one which can only be learned and practiced by those with some degree of clarity and comfort. You can understand that you intrinsically have enough, and that others intrinsically have enough, while working for every waking moment to improve the material conditions of humanity and the planet.

## BE – DO – HAVE ENOUGH

### I Am Enough

The conditioned mind is constantly searching for things to judge as less than or more than enough. Enough is the universal quantity of acceptance. Time, money, energy, and appreciation are among the many concepts that our minds judge as enough, not enough, or too much. The list can go on and on. You created your conditioned mind to help you find enough, but it is born out of the illusion of lack, fear, and entitlement, and can only prevent you from finding enough. It unintentionally causes you to ignore the enough that you already have, and therefore to resist the realization that you are Ten.

Living every day from within the conditioned mind is exhausting. It is The Game Often Played. Within the constant chatter of thoughts in the mind, stories of lack and excess abound. To know that you are Ten, you must know, as a fundamental truth, that you are enough in each moment. To remain in the awareness of Ten, you must let go of your thoughts of the past as well as your thoughts of the future once they are no longer beneficial to your state of mind.

We do not mean to say that you should not have thoughts. Have your thousands of thoughts per day if you wish. Thoughts are only harmful when you attach emotions to them. Use them intentionally and let them go as they came. What brings you Off-Ten is holding onto a thought, usually a positive or negative judgment about a person, thing, or situation. Positive thinking is still a form of judgmental comparison. It still biases your mind toward making judgements of good, bad, better, and worse, which inevitably lead you to degrade yourself or degrade others. The "everything is awesome" mindset will get you to nine in The Game Often Played, but never Ten.

Accepting what is, through present moment awareness, will bring you to Ten and keep you there. It is so simple, yet not easy with our conditioned minds rooted in thought. It may be difficult to accept that you are enough. Especially if a parent, teacher, coach, or any other person of significance has conditioned you to believe that you can always do better.

You are enough as you are right now. It is only when you believe that you are *better-than*, *worse-than*, *more-than* or *less-than*, that the feeling of disappointment from Ten is experienced. When you think you can be better or that you are not being what you or others expect, you are not accepting your-self as you are now.

Create a reset button for yourself wherever you'd like to imagine it. Mine is in the middle of my forehead and I call it F10. It can be your reminder to get back into alignment with Ten. We will say this again: you cannot get to Ten; you already are Ten. The "Aha!" moment of "getting to Ten" is simply the realization that you never left. When you are aware that you are Ten, you know you are always enough for yourself and others, whether or not they choose to be with you.

When a situation or outcome is disappointing or less than you expected, accept that the outcome is still enough, and that you are enough to accept that outcome in stride. If you want a different outcome, raising your awareness and modi-fying your behavior to achieve desired results is what The Game of Ten is all about. The modification begins with constant realization that you are Ten. It is the moment-to-moment realization that you are, always were, and always will be Ten in all ways.

In the mindset of Ten, you cannot want or need to be different. You may think or feel that this is all semantics. Well, it is, and the words themselves only point to the truth. The words that we use and the thoughts that we have can either keep us in the awareness of Ten, or move us closer to, or farther from Ten. Words and thoughts "re-present," presenting different representations of the present moment, leading to a constant repositioning of our awareness and interpretations of the present moment. Your thinking mind is always defining or redefining your concept of *self* in relation to your past and present. You are either aware of it or not. You are either using words from love or words from fear.

*I Do Enough*

The Game of Ten is a tool to bring you to awareness of what *is*. You are not a human doing. You are a human being. How often you forget this. The happy balance between doing too much and too little, is doing *enough* always. Having the awareness to stay in *enough* is often the challenge.

You have always done exactly enough to bring you to your current *life situation* and level of awareness. This will always be the case. What you do is not *who you are* unless your actions are coming from Ten. From Ten, you give and receive without conditions or strings. From Ten you do not, however, deny your own needs in order to give even more to others. Saying, "No, not now," can be very giving and kind when it comes from Ten. You cannot effectively care for others if you never care for yourself; you cannot effectively help yourself or others if you are burnt out from self-sacrifice. You will remain in the awareness of Ten when you *love to do* rather than *have to do*. This is a subtle shift of perception and awareness. *Doing what you love* and *loving what you do* are the keys to knowing that you do enough.

Have you ever noticed that when you love what you are doing, time flies by? It doesn't matter whether it was a great vacation, a book that you could not put down, or a project that you loved. When you are in pure doing, you are in a state of *play*, free from judgmental criticisms of when, why, or how well you are doing it. You are in a zone of timeless, eternal flow.

If you don't have a clear idea of what you love to do, let your openness and awareness guide you to your passion. It requires deep listening in order to hear your calling. You will know you have found it when you experience presence, contentment, and timelessness in what you are doing. The only thing that you can do in The Game of Ten, is to be yourself authentically. All actions from Ten are expressions of your authentic self. This means that you act while accepting yourself as you are, and your situation as it is. In Ten, your "do enough" will remain constant as your life situations change, because you always do enough. Being honest and passionate about what you do is also important to this concept. When you are honest and passionate about what you do, you do your best to show up on the time that you agree upon, and you do your best to fulfill obligations and commitments that you took on. This passion and commitment aligns you with Ten.

> *"I am not the doing.*
> *I am not what is done.*
> *I am the space in which things are done."*
>
> — ECKHART TOLLE

### I Have Enough

When you play The Game of Ten, you always have enough. While the conditioned mind is off chattering about having too much of something bad and not having enough of something good, Ten is sitting back knowing all is right. Everything is all right, right now. At this point, you hopefully understand that The Game of Ten is a mindset that aligns you with awareness. You are resetting your conditioned mind to be aligned with the unconditioned mind.

Quieting the conditioned mind is essential to accessing the unconditioned mind. The Tenets of The Game of Ten are designed to do this. By realizing that you have enough in this moment, awareness kicks in, and you can look beyond the foggy misery of The Game Often Played, to see the opportunities that are available to you.

When you're aware that you have enough, new possibilities become clear. People, things, and situations show up to give you what you have "asked" for and set your intentions for. You must be in a mindset of Ten to recognize that you are getting what you asked for.

When you observe and live your life from this viewpoint of abundance, seeing life as infinitely rich, full of reward, possibilities, and opportunities, you will experience more abundance with every passing day. This is the experience of Ten. So, if you are dissatisfied with your life situation, accept that you are dissatisfied. You now know how to observe, allow, and let go of your thoughts, feelings, and emotions. If you are having difficulty letting them go, take them to an altar you have created in your mind, and be willing to see them differently, and let Ten do what it does best. This act of acceptance and forgiveness will alter your perceptions to bring you back into alignment with Ten. The altar of Ten is "for-giving."

The observing quality of Ten is its main characteristic. Existing as the observing awareness of your inner state is the key to staying in Ten. Your observing awareness exists without needing to think about what is being observed. As soon as you think about what is observed, you become less aware of what *is*. As soon as you judge or self-identify with a thought about what *is*, you separate from Ten. You "become the thinking" and not the observing awareness. You can fall Off-Ten by adding a personalization to your thought, a feeling to your thought, and even attaching a meaning to the thought to make it seem more real and important to you.

Perhaps you're playing The Game of Ten by now, or perhaps you're still watching from the sidelines or the bleachers. Wherever you are in this process, it's right for you at this moment. This is all part of your process of personal development.

Your conditioned mind is trained to think. It interprets the sensory data from awareness into words, thoughts, and judgements, which often provoke feelings unprovoked by the situation itself. You are moving from thought-identification to awareness without self-identification. You are becoming aware of your thoughts and using them, rather than letting them use you.

9

# THE GAME OF TEN

I n this chapter you will read the condensed version of The Game of Ten. It can be downloaded at www. TheGameOfTen.com. Reconditioning your mindset is a repetitive process. You have been reading many of the same concepts repeatedly. This is intentional. Now you will be given more to consider. You will read a remarkable story of Mary Anne Walk's experience using The Game of Ten.

You will be shown how "Words Matter." The words you use in your everyday life have a powerful impact on your mindset. You've come this far and there is more to come. The Game of Ten is a path to a mindset designed to keep you in present moment awareness. You will learn that the universal time is Now, also called Eternity. The universal place is Here, and the universal quantity is Enough. The Tenets that you have learned can also be used as an "active meditation;" you can say throughout the day to bring yourself back into alignment with Ten.

Being aware is also being intuitive. The degree to which you want to embrace and develop your intuition is your choice. As a super parent, your intuition can be invaluable to nurture and guide your child in their journey.

## MARY ANNE'S STORY

In the summer of 2015, after finishing my training at the Gestalt International Study Center, I worked with my former coach Mary Anne Walk via video conference. I became the coach, training and coaching her to increase her intuition. She told me when she hired me that, on a scale of one to Ten, her level of intuition was a seven.

The first thing I said to her in our first coaching session was, "So, you're a seven in your intuition?"

She replied again, "A solid seven."

I said, "Okay, from now on, you are a Ten in your intuition."

After making a face of baffled confusion, she gave a smile and we moved forward. We went over the rules of the game, and I asked her to pay attention to her thoughts, feelings, and emotions as her assignment for the next session. Not to change them, only to pay attention to them.

Between our first and second session, she called me to say that Anders, the brother of her best friend Maria, came over from Sweden to visit New York City. Mary Anne lives across the Hudson River. Anders arrived at her home for a five-day visit. Mary Anne had all her current brochures out from her previous guests who had made day trips to the city.

Remember in Chapter 3, when Mary Anne asked her deceased husband, Ralph, to find her a good man that he approves of? She had made that request long before I had met her. When she mentioned it while her husband was speaking through me, Ralph replied, "I have, he looks like Joe

Garagiola." As I mentioned in Chapter 3, he was a famous baseball player and morning talk show host.

Mary Anne was showing Anders all the places to go in New York City. As Anders watched Marry Anne recite all the amazing sights to see, he took her hand and said, "I didn't come here to see New York City. I came here to see you." This struck her completely by surprise.

When she had a moment to herself, she called me and told me the story and how unexpected it was. They knew each other through Maria, and Mary Anne had known Anders' former wife. Mary Anne, Ralph, Maria, Anders, and Anders' wife had all had dinner together in Sweden years earlier.

Mary Anne said, "But, he doesn't look like Joe Garagiola."

I said, "That is who Ralph picked for you. You pick your own man." We had our third session a week later. We laughed at the unexpected comedy of life and began our session. I don't remember it being very eventful. We talked about how the words we use affect our mindset. After the session, she told me that she was going to Sweden to visit Maria, and to meet Anders' family.

About a week later, I got an email from Mary Anne. It was a photograph of the view from a friend's home: a picturesque meadow sloping toward the Swedish coastline, beyond which sat a small marina and an anchorage dotted with powerboats and sailboats. I replied to the email, saying how beautiful it looked.

A few days later, I received another email, saying, "I'm hearing voices."

My reply was, "You're either crazy or Ten."

She replied, "I'll call you when I get back." When Mary Anne returned, she called me. She had excitement in her voice and a bit of astonishment.

She started with, "Do you remember the picture I sent you?"

"Yes," I replied.

"Well, there was a party for Anders' family to meet me. His children, their spouses, and his grandchildren were all there."

There must have been sixteen people there, all standing on the deck. I decided to get away for a moment to go down below and admire the view alone. Suddenly, I heard a voice, clear as day, saying "turn around." I didn't question it, and I turned around. Then I noticed that my arms were in front of me, like I was carrying a large platter. Within seconds, a fifteen-month-old baby girl landed in my arms. All I could think to say was, 'Got her!' It was a thirteen-foot drop and I was standing on granite. I heard screams of horror from above. That's not all."

Now, I was thinking, What the heck? Mary Anne told me, "A few days later, a dear friend and I were driving down the highway at night. We were in a torrential downpour with glaring lights reflecting off the rain and road. Imagine two big women in a Mini Cooper, with the windshield wipers on high with little to no visibility. Suddenly, the voice came back, it said, 'stop the car now.' I knew if I used those words, my friend would not have stopped the car. So, I reworded it."

I asked, "So, your friend is not a Ten?"

Mary Anne said, "You mean my friend would have still stopped if I used those exact words?"

I said, "Yes."

Mary Anne said, "Well she stopped, thank God. Had she not, we would have been killed. An eighteen-wheeler ran a red light at an intersection just in front of us."

I was amazed at these stories and that she used The Game of Ten. I said, "You have saved the lives of three people in less than a week. Let's take The Game of Ten to your clients in the city."

She said, "Steve, you don't understand. CEOs don't like to play games." At that point, I was about to burst out laughing. From my experience in business, CEOs love to play games, and they particularly love to *win*.

I said, "I'll talk with you tomorrow."

I hung up the phone and rolled on the floor laughing. It was a laugh of relief that The Game of Ten works. I was grateful for the lives that were saved, grateful for Mary Anne's dedication, and grateful that the method which helped me could truly help others.

The next day I gave Mary Anne a call. The first thing I said was, "So, CEOs don't like to play games?"

She said with excitement in her voice, "Steve, you have something here. I don't know what it is, but you have something. This is a great process to use with clients and you have something."

Mary Anne is now one of my dearest friends and mentors. Currently, she travels between the US and Sweden to be with Anders, and Anders often comes to New Jersey. I called a few months ago, on FaceTime. Mary Anne was in Sweden, and Anders walked by. Mary Anne asked me, "Hey do you want to meet Anders?"

I said, "Yes!"

She said with laughter in her voice, "My friends think he looks like Joe Garagiola."

There was a strong resemblance. We chatted and laughed about how they got together. I said to Anders, "You're a lucky man to have Mary Anne in your life and I can tell she is just as lucky to have you in hers."

We talked again a month later. Mary Anne and Anders were out for a walk in Sweden. She brought up the fact that she has been with Anders for over five years. I could tell by her voice, how happy she was and said, "Your husband Ralph picked you a good one."

She said, "He certainly did."

In my opinion, this story is an example of what you may call divine intervention and guidance. It is always available to you and yet often people do not live in the state of stillness and awareness to access it.

I tell you this story because it demonstrates the power that you have within you. You need only be willing to allow it into our mind. There are many stories of life saving miracles, of people performing extraordinary feats when extraordinary situations arise. Even the seemingly mundane events that occur in everyday life can come to be seen as amazing. Like spending time being present with your child.

## THE GAME OF TEN®

### What Is The Game of Ten?

The Game of Ten is a tool to help people understand and achieve awareness of themselves and the world around them. It is a set of principles meant to increase one's capacity to accept life as it is, while promoting self-acceptance and fulfillment.

### What Is Ten?

Ten is the highest point on the scale of acceptance of what is. Ten is used in this context to describe pure awareness and unconditional love.

## What Is Awareness?

Awareness is the awake, alive, and original state of being. In many ways, to *be* is to *be aware*. It is the state of mind of no thought, or only of loving thoughts derived from awareness. Loving thoughts keep us aligned with Ten. All unloving thoughts separate us from awareness. The conditioned mind hijacks the unconditioned mind through fear and self-identification, leading to thoughts and feelings of separateness from Ten.

## What Is the Conditioned Mind?

We think our thoughts are real. They are a creation of the conditioned mind. You will know if they are of this mind, if the thought is derived from fear, or is unloving toward a person or situation. This is also a collective phenomenon. Awareness is real. Observing thoughts derived from present moment awareness is as close to what is real as the conditioned mind will ever let you experience. Yet, thinking aware thoughts is not itself an act of awareness. "Pure" awareness exists before, beneath, and in the absence of thought and judgment.

We are born with unconditioned minds. Through our experiences over time, we are conditioned into habits, patterns, thoughts, feelings, emotions, and behaviors. The first and most noticeable of these patterns and behaviors: the conditioned mind, builds structures, patterns and thought forms from awareness (which is formless) because the conditioned mind thinks awareness needs support. It does not. Language, emotion, self-identity, and fear, are ingredients for what most of us see as our "self." We refer to this mind-made self-concept as the ego, in the sense of the phrases "feed your ego" and "ego death" rather than in the Freudian sense.

Comparisons drive the conditioned mind. The conditioned mind deals in duality, degrees, and polarities. The most common and destructive comparisons are: what is good and what is bad? What is right and what is wrong? What is enough and what is not?

First comes your personalization of a thought, thinking: "my thought, my idea" or "I think." Then comes emotional attachment to a feeling and emotion, how you feel about a person or situation. It will be derived from fear.

## THE GAME OF TEN

### *Rules of the Game, the Extended List of Tenets*

- I am Ten
- Everyone is also Ten
- I am always right with the awareness I have
- I am doing the best I can with the awareness I have
- Everyone is always right with the awareness they have
- Everyone is doing the best they can with the awareness they have
- I am enough
- I do enough
- I have enough
- Everyone is enough
- Everyone does enough
- Everyone has enough

*Be- Do- Have*

- *Being* is awareness
- *Doing* is action from awareness
- *Having* is the result of setting intentions from awareness

*Be-Have*

- Follow the rules
- Do what you love
- Love what you do
- Doing becomes playing

When playing The Game of Ten, you are to have no attachment to your thoughts, emotions, feelings, or sensations. They all will be heightened when you detach your self-identification from them and allow them to flow independently.

### Present Moment Awareness

When you are playing The Game of Ten, you are in present moment awareness.

The rules of the game are designed to quiet the mind.

## WHAT IS FEAR?

- The only thing you can fear is Love
- Your true arrogance is thinking and feeling that you are anything other than connected with the aspects of Ten
- Your guilt is the feeling that you did something bad
- Your shame is the thought that you are bad
- Your guilt, shame, fear, and doubt, are hooks by which fear brings you Off-Ten

In The Game of Ten, you become Off-Ten whenever you play The Game Often Played. You can believe that you are less-than or better-than a person or situation, but also whenever you experience and cling to fear, suffering, or anger. Hooks elicit reactions when your thoughts are clouded and emotional. Part of avoiding clouded and emotional thought patterns means taking care of yourself, meeting your physical needs for sufficient food and sleep. A good method to reduce your susceptibility to hooks involves reciting the Tenets until they become natural to you.

## THE GAME OFTEN PLAYED: ONE TO NINE

- I am not Ten
- You/ we/ they are not Ten
- I am not right with the awareness I have
- I am not doing the best I can with the awareness I have
- They are not right with the awareness they have
- They are not doing the best they can with the awareness they have

- I am not enough
- You/ we/ they are not enough
- I don't do enough
- You/ we/ they don't do enough
- I don't have enough
- You/ we/ they don't have enough

You are not always mad, sad, or scared for the reasons you *think* that you are. You get mad, sad, and scared because you get hooked and separated from alignment with Ten. Now that you are aware of what gets you Off-Ten, how do you become aware and get back to playing Ten?

### Tens Set Intentions

Your behaviors, when aligned with your intentions, promote intended results. Intentions from awareness, and actions from awareness, lead to favorable results. When you are playing The Game of Ten, you are appointed Ten. You cannot be dis-appointed from Ten until your thoughts, feelings or emotions cause you to become "hooked."

## WHAT IS A HOOK?

To see "peace" or "enlightenment" as a state a human being can constantly maintain, seems rather unrealistic. In The Game of Ten, when a thought or situation drags you Off-Ten, we call it a "hook." Everybody is always intrinsically Ten. Sometimes, however, our minds are hooked by a thought about being Off-Ten. Hooks can catch you off guard, and their barbed tips make them hard to remove. Common emotional hooks involve criticisms and rude comments made by yourself or others. If any of the rules of

The Game Often Played ring true for you, then you will be hooked.

The moment you believe one of the rules of The Game Often Played, you are Off-Ten. The more of these thoughts and beliefs you have, the further away from Ten you will feel, and the more guilt and shame you will have around these thoughts. Bringing these thoughts and feelings to awareness is essential to releasing them. Being Off-Ten is situational. It depends on one's internal and external situation.

When you are Off-Ten, you become *mad, sad, and scared*, and generally take it out on yourself or others. You might say that you are temporarily insane and willing to share your insanity with others. In truth, even taking something out on others still takes it out on yourself, just with a minor detour of becoming the oppressor and victim of others around you as well.

Your hooks attach to emotional wounds from your conditioned past. They can snag onto you and pull you out of awareness, dragging you Off-Ten. Hooks are things that people and situations say or do to you, often your own thoughts or feelings can hook into you as well. They reel in thoughts that you are not *right, enough,* or Ten. When you get hooked in the game, you think that you are Off-Ten, and you begin to feel, mad, sad, and scared.

They could come in the form of criticisms from authority figures, family members, or trusted peers. Hooks often tap into the deep human need for in-group acceptance, and the equally instinctual fear of rejection. Hooks are therefore different from "triggers" in the sense that triggers relate to specific personal traumas like surviving violence, oppression, or abandonment. Hooks react with the unconscious mind and nervous system in similar ways to triggers, but it does not require past trauma in order to be hooked and brought Off-Ten.

Our bodies can trap fear, stress, and hatred in very deep parts of the brain and nervous system; parts which are only exposed in times of similar fear, stress, and hatred. In The Game of Ten, these deeply conditioned impulses can be seen as part of the conditioned mind, albeit closer to reflexes, and harder to retrain than your resting thought patterns.

OBSERVE-FEEL-ALLOW-RELEASE

- Observe the hook
- Feel the hook
- Allow the hook
- It will release over time

The Game of Ten provides an opportunity to remove your hooks once and for all; at the very least, you will have the tools to release them as they arise. As you become hooked less frequently, you will more consistently remain in alignment with Ten. By remaining in Ten, you will find present moment awareness, flow, love, the zone, bliss, inner peace, abundance, truth, compassion, intuition, atonement, absolution, and much more. Hooks will release over time as you accept that your ego has lied to you, that you have lied to yourself.

*"Awareness is our common sense, the sense that connects us all as one."*

— STEVE BARTON

## WORDS MATTER

Your thoughts and words are powerful things. The words you use are powerful, in the sense that they can affect your mindset. Below are some words and phrases that you may consider reducing your usage of or avoiding altogether. At first, just be aware that you are using them. The more aware you are of their usage, the more you will develop the ability to rephrase or transcend them.

### Destructive Words

*(Words to be aware that you are using and thinking.)* Depending on their usage, some words and thoughts are constructive, and others are destructive. These words fuel destructive thoughts.

### Guilt-Shame-Blame Words

- Should
- Would
- Could
- Ought to
- Blame
- Fault
- I'm sorry

### Lack Words

- Need
- Want
- Not enough
- Miss

*Entitlement Words*

- Worthy
- Owe
- Deserve

*Words That Sound Great and (Can) Keep Us from Ten*

- Belief
- Faith
- Hope

*Non-Words*

- Try

*Defeatist Words*

- Can't
- Won't

Some words like "wrong" can mean morally wrong, or factually incorrect, and it becomes a context-dependent destructive word. The same goes for "try" which can simply mean "to apply effort," but which often leads people to define their self-worth based on their abilities. Likewise, belief, faith, and hope sound great, but imply it is bad or wrong to not share in a particular belief, faith, or hope, while also implying that there is no evidence for having belief, faith, or hope – context matters. If you'd like to, you can experiment with noticing these words for an hour, day, or week. See how your worldview changes when you remove these destructive words from daily usage as much as possible.

Look inside to see what is going on. Observe what you think and feel when you or others are speaking these words. Be respectful of others in their word usage. Only correct or inform them when they ask you to do so.

### Choice and Preference Words

It is popular in today's psychology, coaching, self-help, and wellness community to say that choice is the highest level of freedom. Choice, choosing, and preference are a step up from destructive words. It can be tempting to think that the choice is yours to make. However, the choices you make from thought, rather than awareness, will always come with some degrees of lessons to be learned. You are always doing the best you can with the awareness you have. To dwell on past and future choices can lead to far more suffering than could be prevented by making a "better choice." Surrender your thoughts to presence and awareness. It is the only choice, and not a choice at all.

### Level Ten Words (Accepting, Loving, Constructive)

- Unconditional Love
- Peace
- Happiness
- Health
- Wholeness
- Joy
- Enough
- Here
- Right, now
- Eternal
- Presence

- Absolution
- Allowance
- Truth
- Knowledge
- Wisdom
- Power
- Awareness
- Appreciation
- Gratitude
- Grace
- Giving
- Receiving
- Acceptance
- Inclusion
- Forgiveness

You can be sure there are many more. These words and concepts can help you to improve your mindset and stay in The Game of Ten. Let Ten (awareness) make the choices for you. The mindset of Ten is presented to you. Ask from this level. Be patient and compassionate with yourself (and your sense of self). Your life is happening for *you* every day *you* allow it to.

Did you ever take the time in your life to do such a mental and emotional inventory? Well, you have come very far, and you have taken a lot in. You have learned the games and hopefully will practice the concepts and tools for yourself. You have learned that words matter. They are to be used intentionally, for you are an intentional being using words to express love. Express this love to yourself, your child, and the people you encounter in your daily life.

*Be deliberate with your words.*

- The universal quantity is enough
- The universal space is here
- The universal time is now
- The universal awareness is right

These powerful words can be swapped around to fit the situation you are in.

They are powerfully directive for a reason:

- The time is right
- Be here right now
- Enough is enough
- Here is here
- Right is right

The quantity, space, and time of awareness is enough, right here, right now.

You can go on and on. These are absolute words. To have peace of mind, your awareness must be aligned with them.

# WHAT IS HOLDING YOU BACK
# FROM PLAYING?

Nothing you can perceive about the world is perfectly "real" but that's okay. The feelings of pain, fear, and love are all just stories that part of your brain tells the rest of it. To us, the meaning of life is choosing which of those stories and experiences matter and choosing *love* every time.

## LOVE, PAIN, AND FEAR

Pain is one of the most primal sensory signals, and fear is just the internalization and preemption of perceived pain by the primal elements of the brain. Love, however, is slightly less primal, but much more powerful when used responsibly. It is the basis for humanity's cooperation and success, and we believe the capability to love is the best case for humanity's continued existence. Statements like "love is stronger than fear" are certainly comforting in a fairytale kind of way, but they ignore that the "pure ideal forms" of love and fear are not faced by humans during their lifetimes. They are feelings experienced in degrees, a spectrum, not a binary.

Fear can appear to be stronger than love. Love is stronger than fear. We would argue that love is smarter than fear and leads people to act in the common interest, meanwhile fear is more insidious than love. Fear can grab hold of people's minds and make them act in irrational and horribly selfish ways, with enough fear and indoctrination, it can lead people to callously commit atrocities. There are many reasons why people will get to work on time. All of them can be traced back to either love of an intrinsically meaningful and rewarding experience, or fear of a punishment.

The world is more complex than our brains are capable of comprehending, and not just because they are, themselves, part of it; but the world of human beings is far more knowable and reducible, one need only understand empathy and interpersonal dynamics, and be in the proper mental and physical state to respond from awareness.

## WHAT YOU RESIST PERSISTS

We have had an amazing journey developing The Game of Ten, and we hope it will aid you on your own amazing journey to come. Hopefully, Spencer and I have successfully prepared you to play The Game of Ten® and to notice when you are playing The Game Often Played. We expect that we've explained things you already knew or suspected, but hopefully we've explained them in a way that you have not heard before.

If you have taken the leap to Ten, you will encounter resistance within yourself and others. This is "normal." You are challenging the beliefs within yourself, your family, and society. Change never comes easily; yet it's so worth it when it gives you peace of mind and happiness in all areas of your life.

You are moving from normal to natural. By moving into this new mindset, you're not becoming "better" or "more," you're moving into who you are and always have been. Your conditioned mind will resist this at all costs. It simultaneously thinks it's you, and fears its demise. We assure you it will always be waiting in the darkness for an opportunity to be well-intentioned but consistently harmful.

Use the Tenets from The Game of Ten as an active mantra and meditation. Use them throughout the day. They cannot be overused. As you train your mind, you will find over time that you will use the Tenets less than when first reconditioning your mind. Also understand that the words of the Tenets are not actually "Ten" themselves. They are assumptions which prepare your mindset and allow your formless awareness to work through you, in alignment with your true nature. You have always been Ten; you most likely weren't aware of it. Also be aware that everyone is Ten and everything is also Ten, otherwise you will fall back into The Game Often Played.

TENETS

*I am Ten.*
*I am always right with the awareness I have.*
*I am always doing the best I can with the awareness I have.*
*I am enough.*
*I do enough.*
*I have enough.*

Know that your tenacious mind, (aka ego, conditioned mind) hates these words because it uses the opposite to do its job, to make you think and feel that you are less than Ten.

We created the Tenets of The Game of Ten as a mantra to quiet the mind. The tenacious mind "speaks first and loudest." When it comes in, don't fall into the trap of pushing it away. It loves to hate you and be hated by you; this will only enhance its illusory control over you. You simply watch it, allow it, and observe it, surrender to it and bring its story to the altar of Ten for it to be altered by your higher self.

You may wonder why you would ever surrender to the tenacious, egoic, Off-Ten mind, brought about by The Game Often Played. The reason is: you can't beat it at its own game. It's not because it's more powerful than you, it's because you created it, and you have taught it your deepest fears and desires. It's The Game Often Played, and you can't win.

So, don't play with it. It knows how to beat you because it knows your fears. It *is* your fears. It beats you emotionally and physically in untold ways. It cannot, however, beat you spiritually because it is not a product of your innate self, or of Ten. Your mind created it and Ten will never undo what you have created through your thoughts unless you are willing to invite it in to do so. When invited in, the awareness of Ten has the ability and willingness to heal your mind of unloving, and painful thoughts. When you ask, and are willing to see people, things, and situations differently, this can be called a prayer.

When playing The Game Often Played, your thoughts can still control you, and your awareness and contentment can only be expressed up to nine. This can be achieved through "positive thinking." The Off-Ten mind will never willingly allow you to reach and experience the awareness of Ten. Circuits require both positive and negative charges, though these are not related to "good" or "bad" the way negative thoughts are. For electrical energy to flow within, the circuit must be complete. For awareness to flow through us, we must be willing to both accept and release our thoughts, feelings, and experiences. Even if you get to nine, the circuit will have a loose connection. This is because the tenacious mind, so long as you continue to listen to it, can only ever bring you close to Ten. Because the tenacious mind is innately fearful, it will never let you experience Ten.

You will see things differently when playing The Game of Ten. It is a 180-degree rotation, a paradigm shift from The Game Often Played. It is the end of the paradoxes of duality, karma, and the fear-based mindset. It all gets dissolved into a love-based mindset.

With this new way of being, you may have many different experiences that come with it, it depends how far Off-Ten you were or are. The farther Off-Ten, the more resistance you will be experiencing. Just practice observing, allowing, and releasing it, as we discussed earlier. This resistance is "normal." Take your time. The transition from normal to natural will happen when you are ready. Remember this resistance is your fear of love, and it is your power coming back to you.

Do you understand how accepting love over fear will make you a great parent to your child? Ultimately, we cannot predict what your experience with The Game of Ten will entail. From our experience, the more you remain Ten throughout your daily life, the more you will experience the miracles and "Aha!" moments that occur throughout it.

I remember, in 1992, when I had my out-of-body/ near-death experience. My life was not the same from that moment on, as you have read. There was a lot of resistance from some of my family toward the changes they saw in me, and they wanted the "old" Steve back. Let me assure you that their reaction was on the extreme end of things. I have learned to only share this information with people who are willing to ask about it (this book notwithstanding). The results of these changes have been wonderful and have led me to forming deeper relationships with others in my life.

I have also let go of people in my life who don't see life as I see it. Be prepared for that. You will see that some people, behaviors, and situations no longer benefit you. This may be what you are resisting. The ones that want to hold you back are afraid you will leave them. They may say "I don't get you now. I don't like this change in you. I don't like you now that you have changed." True, change for the better or worse is subjective, but an increase in awareness means an improvement in the ability to direct the process of change itself. Awareness comes when you surrender the fearful desire for control, yet, paradoxically, it allows you greater control.

Remember, the ones that do this are Ten, yet are not aware of it. They are playing The Game Often Played. It is not our place to "change" them, ever. The most unloving behavior toward yourself and others is wanting someone to be different than they are now.

They are doing the best they can with the awareness they have. You can only stay in Ten if you see every human in this way (indeed, it holds true for animals and many complex systems as well). It is a declaration of your innocence and of theirs. When we see someone as guilty, we also see ourselves as guilty. You will be thrown back to The Game Often Played, until you let go of your guilt, and the guilt and shame of others.

Now don't think for a minute that loving everyone and everything and seeing yourself and everyone else as Ten, is going to make you a wet noodle, it does quite the opposite. You will be able to keep your heart open. This is its natural state. You will also be able to have clear boundaries with people and situations that come into your life.

We have found that by staying in Ten, the need for boundaries is not often used. We respect other people's personal and social boundaries and by doing so ours are respected. Some are less fortunate and must fight for their boundaries to be respected. Sometimes love says yes. Sometimes love says no. Sometimes love says stay. Sometimes love says go.

So, stay true to yourself always, and be kind to others who are on their own journeys to awareness. Remember, you must love them, you don't have to be with them. Remembering this is the most loving thing you can do for yourself and others.

## SPENCER'S STORY

This book has been years in the making. My father and I have shared many interesting discussions about these concepts and how best to refine them for the reader. Over the years, we've also seen some of the phrases we use enter more mainstream use. We acknowledge that none of our ideas occurred in a vacuum. We have been influenced by some, we have arrived at some concepts independently, and we have influenced others. Most of this book is written by my father, but I have also made many multiple-paragraph long additions and numerous corrections, clarifications, and continuity improvements. I believe that my father has lived a life worth writing about and developed methods with the ability to help many people understand and improve upon their thought patterns, and thereby improve upon their actions and their quality of life.

This writing process has felt drawn out at times and very rushed at others. I'll admit I had hoped to read and research far more on our topics of discussion than I was able to. With all our ideas, notes, and now our experience writing a book, we quite possibly have more on the way.

As I write these words, I'm still a teenager, still living with my mother. I never expected to write a book about parenting. This book is written by a father and a son and indeed marketed toward parents, but the methods we use for finding peace and understanding with oneself and others are universal. We have all been children. As adults, we still carry many of our memories and conditioned responses from child-hood. In some ways, growing up means taking on the roles of self-care, maintenance, and self-direction previously managed (effectively or otherwise) by parental figures. I mean to say, whether or not you are currently parenting others, you never stopped parenting yourself.

Our discussions of worldview, self-talk, and mindset within this book are meant to illuminate how you can over-come your own harmful conditioning, while making sure you are not passing harmful conditioning on to others.

My father often uses words like real, truth, knowing, thought, and spirit in unconventional ways. Statements made within this work should be taken in the context of this book as a whole. At their core, the ideas my father puts forth can be agreeable to many, whether theists, atheists, spiritualists, or materialists. Peering past spiritual language, there is often psychological truth.

My father will occasionally make claims like "time isn't real" or "The Game of Ten is about spacetime" which are only potentially true when interpreted in very specific contexts. For example, the claim "time isn't real" can have many different meanings, since *"time," "isn't,"* and *"real,"* can all be taken to mean different things in different contexts. In this case, I believe my father means something closer to "It's never not now. Memories are subjective, and the future isn't a real thing because it's always just the present." On the spacetime claim, I'm not ashamed to disagree with my father. I see The Game of Ten as a framework to help people remain present and peaceful within their minds; meaning that it helps them to feel and have enough in the here and now. The fact that *here* is a point in space, and *now* is a point in time, is about the extent to which I believe spacetime factors into the game.

The Game of Ten also presents a new way of seeing relativity between concepts. Even someone who embraces nihilism or moral relativism may still experience fear, guilt, shame, and self-doubt. The rules of The Game of Ten go a step further, saying: whether or not there is any objective meaning or purpose, wouldn't it be nice to find peace and contentment? Instead of stopping at "my thoughts, feelings, hopes and fears don't objectively matter," The Game of Ten understands that just because someone can rationalize that something is neutral, doesn't mean they automatically feel at peace with that thing. It's healthy and natural to feel emotions. Humans would not have evolved them to their present degree had they not served some advantage. It is, however, unhealthy to dwell on painful emotions while discounting pleasurable ones, as worrying and self-deprecation often lead to. You need only accept that peace and pleasure are preferable to pain and suffering. From there, remind yourself that you are enough, you do enough, and you have enough. You are always right with the awareness you have, and you are always doing the best you can with the awareness you have. When you know that, then you will always know that you are Ten. When you play the game, you *accept* that you are Ten, whether or not you *feel* that you are Ten. You accept that everyone else is Ten, whether or not you feel love or hatred toward them. This helps you to accept your thoughts and emotions as both real experiences and as separate from objective reality, which in turn helps you to separate your sense of self from your thoughts and separate your thoughts from your feelings. This is, in truth, more respectful to your sense of self, your thoughts, and your feelings, because you no longer let any one of them dominate the others.

All of this has been said many times, in many ways. It is my hope that our writing and my father's method will find those who are most in need of these realizations. If any quiet parts remained, it is my greatest hope that we've said them out loud.

While lacking peace and contentment is detrimental your health, nothing will bring you to inner peace and general happiness more effectively than improvement to your mental and physical health. As the mind is a function of the physical brain, mental health is also a physical phenomenon with physical influences, such as nutrition, blood sugar, blood oxygen, nervous system stimulation, neurotransmitter levels, and much more. The Game of Ten prevented me from mentally punishing myself for my academic failings, but it did not prevent the chronic stress, fatigue, and sleep deprivation that came with my undiagnosed ADHD in a high-intensity college-prep environment. Everyone is doing the best they can with the awareness they have and, as an author, I will do my best to raise awareness of what has helped me to live a healthy and happy life. Although we believe mindset to be a cornerstone of healthy and happy living, it still requires healthy living.

Testing, diagnosis, and medication for ADHD has been the biggest recent improvement in my quality of life. I was eighteen years old, but many adults are diagnosed very late in their lives. Most people wish they had been diagnosed and treated a lot earlier. When people start ADHD medication, they often quit their addictive or dependency-inducing substances and activities, because they finally have the neurochemicals which they were always unconsciously trying to get their fill of.

Beyond that, consistent, deep sleep, consistent physical activity including cardio, a diet with few or no processed foods, particularly processed sugars, limited caffeine and alcohol use, frequent cognitively stimulating tasks, and time with friends, family, loved ones, and community, will all benefit the human mind and body.

A major premise of this book is the ability of thoughts and assumptions to shape human feelings and behaviors. I believe it is important to discuss how comfortable delusions are often easier for people to hold than uncomfortable truths. We hope that The Game of Ten allows people to take comfort in truths they would otherwise deny out of fear. Unfortunately, moving beyond fear does not necessarily require moving beyond wishful and delusional thinking. You can know that you are right with the awareness you have, but not know just how far you truly are from understanding reality. Delusion can be caused by denial or unawareness of what is. To move fully beyond delusion requires both fearlessness, and complete awareness (knowledge) of reality. The concept of truth is only relative insofar as it is a value that can only exist in constellation with other statements which are taken to be true. In science, our best tool for finding truth about the physical world, the concept of truth is unnecessarily clunky, loaded with moralistic and deterministic assumptions. In scientific language, a well-established theory that is based on experimentation and evidence, and creates accurate predictions about the world, is what we could call a scientific truth. It is a statement or model which holds true for a given set of circumstances, like a group of finches adapting over successive generations to live on an island (Darwin's theory of evolution) or an object accelerating toward the ground when dropped (the theory of gravity).

I believe my father still holds some wishful thinking and untested assumptions. I would not be a good skeptic if I didn't admit that I may hold my own wishful thinking and untested assumptions, though I do my best to be vigilant and open-minded.

Introducing cryptic terminology is often a tool used by grifters to convince unscrupulous onlookers that they have access to rare or secret knowledge, and can share it with you, so long as you buy their course or other nonsense. We have done our best to avoid vague language during this writing process, but vagueness and abstraction come with the territory of discussing mindset and systems of thought. The Game of Ten® is a registered trademark belonging to my father, and it introduces the term Ten which refers to a mindset of awareness and acceptance of oneself and one's environment. We use terms like awareness, ego, and conditioned mind, in a similar manner as they are used by A Course in Miracles, The Gestalt International Study Center, and by bestselling author Eckhart Tolle.

Something can be both timeless and eternal because eternal means without end, and the present moment, "now" is both a point which is never any longer, shorter, later, or sooner, and which also never ends. A particular moment ends, but we only ever experience the endless present moment.

Simplicity is the sign of a good theory. In this case, my father took a simple theory of the assumptions behind negative thought patterns and turned it into a set of assumptions which show negative thoughts to be illogical, if not unthinkable. Likewise, the Tenets of The Game of Ten seem illogical when you are playing The Game Often Played.

A unified theory is only a sensible goal in a system with mechanistic and describable phenomena. Human thought is often full of contradictions, so the Tenets of the game provide a framework for observing one's own thoughts; a comprehensive viewpoint with the benefit of reflecting reality and promoting peace of mind.

Don't worry if you cannot yet escape The Game Often Played. Not only have years of conditioning strengthened the thought patterns surrounding it, but many people have environmental stressors and physical predispositions which bias their bodies and minds toward anxiety, depression, aggression, and numerous other psychological responses, each of which sets the mental stage for attempts to rationalize and justify these responses, as well as promoting further suffering, guilt, shame, and fear induced by worry and excessive thinking.

Pain is a real experience. Suffering is a real experience. We simply claim that The Game of Ten can help people avoid the prolonged suffering of guilt, shame, worry, and self-doubt, by showing that these are not based in reality, but based in illusions created by fear.

The Game of Ten begins where many traditions of mindfulness have left off. You know you must be present; you know your thoughts are unhealthy, but you may still believe your thoughts. It's okay to need a replacement mindset to fall back on when your mind happens to leave the present moment.

Admittedly the themes of parenting within this book are not as strong as those of mindfulness and mindset. We set out to make a book for a specific audience (current parents) while our methods were developed with a general adult audience in mind. We are both sons, but only one of us is a father, and we have been hesitant to give general parenting advice based only on our specific experiences.

We are, however, father-and-son co-authors, and my father successfully explained these concepts to me when I was twelve years old. Frankly, I was ready for them much earlier. I credit The Game of Ten for allowing me to overcome or lessen my emotional struggles throughout school and beyond. I credit it with improving my quality of life as much as, or more than, starting a gluten-free diet at age nine, and starting ADHD treatment at age eighteen. Given that the other two issues were hereditary, an improvement in mindset has been the greatest gift to me that I believe everyone has the capacity to receive. I hope my father and I have effectively shared this gift with you. Children are impressionable and adaptable. At the age of twelve, it took me a month of consciously observing, feeling, allowing, and releasing my thoughts and feelings before I was consistently aware and self-aware. Who knows how much easier it would have been if I had begun a few years earlier?

Perhaps those most likely to need this book are least likely to read this. This may be true, but in our experience sharing these ideas, most people can gain something profound from these pages. Perhaps the best way to reach the people most in need, is to reach as many people as possible, so if you enjoyed this book, spread the word, share it with others, if you hated the book, give it to someone you hate, maybe they'll find something you didn't. If they learn anything from this book, we hope they learn how not to take things personally.

We have all done the best we can with the time, energy, knowledge, resources, and awareness we have. Even if our main advice wasn't parenting-specific, I hope we've presented ideas which you can integrate and practice within your own life and share with the young people in your life who are open to it. Young people are the future, and by our presence, we make the future.

> *"The ultimate, hidden truth of the world is that it is something that we make, and could just as easily make differently."*

> — DAVID GRAEBER

# ARE WE THERE YET?

We hope you enjoyed reading *The Father, the Son, and the Aha Moment*. We wish you many "Aha!" moments using the tools of The Game of Ten to help you and your child develop a path to happiness. The starting point of a satisfied life is realizing you are already at the finish line and never separated from your wholeness in the first place. Love can't change the past, but it's the only way to improve the future.

Please use this book to guide yourself and your child to awareness. You are a powerful influence in your child's life. You now possess some new knowledge and tools, which few parents have access to. Your personal body of knowledge makes you capable of synthesizing new ideas unique in human history. Knowledge and awareness are the basis for new insights and creativity.

You are resilient. You've had no choice but to be. Some days you or others may not see that resilience, but it's none-theless there. You are always doing the best you can with the awareness you have, even if you aren't consciously aware of all the effort you're putting in.

You are present. You are right here, right now, reading this. Whether or not you exist for a reason, you are reading this for a reason. You have a reason why you are reading this rather than reading or doing anything else, and that is amazing. Whether or not your reasons are short-term or long-term, whether the pieces of your life currently appear scattered or well-fitting, they are connected. When you read this book, when you go to bed early and wake up refreshed, all of these will contribute to the totality of personal growth which will make far more sense in hindsight and will conspire to remind you that there's no time like the present, and no time for action except the present.

As a parent, you know the challenges of wanting to be the best possible caregiver for your child. It can be difficult to support and guide a young person as they develop their self-awareness, as well as their awareness and acceptance of others. Learn to play The Game of Ten, practice it, and share these ideas with your child if they are receptive. Remember, if you attempt to teach someone The Game of Ten out of a desire to make them different, rather than out of love for them, you may have more to learn.

You have been introduced to me and Spencer, and we hope you have found some of these stories compelling, and some stranger than fiction. The way we see it, you can't make this stuff up. Hopefully it will help you to understand events in your life that you may have been unable to explain, as they may have been too bizarre to even tell.

You were introduced to The Game Often Played and The Game of Ten. You learned that your thoughts have power, and the words you say and think matter as well. You have learned concepts which can stay with you every day. You have discovered tools to help you see things differently; tools to help you forgive, accept, love, and find happiness in your life, and to help your child do the same.

## MAGGIE'S STORY

We want to share one more story with you. It's about Maggie. The same weekend that I channeled Mary Anne's husband Ralph; I was returning to Maine from The Gestalt International Study Center. I stopped at the rest area in Kennebunkport to grab a bite to eat.

While there, I ran into Jean, she was new to a non-profit board that I have been on for years. It is a curated 18th century Victorian home unlike any in the United States. Jean is highly educated in museum science. I really didn't know her very well; I knew that I liked her and wanted to get to know her more. We planned to have coffee the following Thursday.

I returned home, and the following morning I heard a voice in my mind. It said, "My name is Maggie. My name is Maggie." Throughout the days leading up to my meeting with Jean, the voice was relentless. I would say to it, "Yes, I know your name is Maggie, what can I do for you?" All Maggie would say was, "My name is Maggie." This went on for days.

The day finally came to have coffee with Jean. I got in my car to drive to the coffee shop to meet Jean. In the back seat was the cutest little old lady. I couldn't "see" her per se; I just knew what she looked like and what she was wearing. She had curly red hair, a Kelly-green boiled wool jacket, a knee-length skirt, opaque stockings, and black Mary Jane shoes.

She began clapping her hands together while gleefully repeating, "We're going to see my Jeannie! We're going to see my Jeannie!" The mystery of Maggie was beginning to unfold, hinting at who she was and who she was there to see.

I arrived at the coffee shop, and I wasn't quite sure how to talk to Jean about what had been going on with Maggie. We got our coffees and began getting to know each other. About fifteen minutes into our conversation, I came out and said, "Do you know a Maggie?" I described her to Jean with the details that I had. Jean replied, "She's, my grandmother." Jean and her grandmother were very close, and we talked about her memories about her.

Jean and I became instant friends, and we made a lunch date for a few weeks after we met for coffee. I didn't hear any more from Maggie until I was on the street of the restaurant where we planned to have lunch.

In the back seat was Maggie again. This time she was bragging about how smart Jean was and all her degrees and accomplishment that she had achieved. Then she said to me, "I can help you write your book. I'm a beautiful writer."

I arrived at the restaurant and said to Jean, "Guess who showed up in the back seat again?" Jean smiled and said, "Maggie?" I replied, "She was bragging all about you and then she was touting her writing abilities." Jean said, "Oh Steve, she wrote the most beautiful letters. I saved them all in a box. I just can't get rid of them."

I haven't heard from Maggie since, yet I'm sure she is around. My girlfriend's son moved in with us six months ago from South Carolina. He brought his dog with him to live here with him. Her name is Maggie.

Jean hired me to help her with an intense international project she was working on. I called her to ask if I could tell this story. I asked If it was helpful with the process I used with her, The Game of Ten. She said it was very helpful in keeping her in a mindset of, "I can do this."

We tell these stories to let you know that as a parent raising your child, anything is possible when you are open to the possibilities. The journey to awareness can be sudden for some and gradual for others, and in some rare cases you've always been there, and this book is an affirmation of this. Whatever your experience has been while reading this book, we are sure that you have never read this information presented in this way before.

There is a lot inside and outside of our lives that we are not aware of, and we offer this book as a guide for when life presents itself in ways you never imagined. We hope that you use these lessons, stories, and tools to help you through your journey of everyday living, growing up, parenting, and more.

# ACKNOWLEDGMENTS

## FROM STEVE AND SPENCER

We would like to thank and acknowledge all the people in our lives who have brought us to where we are today. To our friends and family, thank you for teaching us the meanings of forgiveness, kindness, and love.

To The Author Incubator team: Special thanks again to Dr Angela Lauria, CEO and founder of The Author Incubator for believing in us and our message. To my developmental editor, Madeline Victoria, and managing editor, Cory Hott, thanks for making the process seamless and easy. Many more thanks to everyone else at TAI, but especially Ramses, Karmi, Jasmine, Lesley, and Nina. Your dedication and drive to make us do our best in this writing process were and are very much appreciated. You provided the educational tools to write this book. Without them, this book would not have been possible.

## FROM SPENCER

To my father, for fostering my love of long conversations and abstract concepts, for including me in this project despite my difficulties finding and managing time, and for understanding that when I am insistent or opinionated, it means I care.

To my mother, for her care, kindness, and flexibility, as we were cleaning and remodeling her house and my sudden involvement in this writing project meant that I left parts of the house messy for months longer than expected.

FROM STEVE

To Spencer for taking on this assignment of being my son and coauthor of our first book. Without him, this book would not be what it is. Thank you for your opinions, insights, and knowledge of the topic and your ability to put it into words. You are and will always be my AHA moment and my lifelong lesson in love, compassion, understanding, and kindness.

To Marianne Williamson for being a mentor from the beginning, thirty years ago whether you knew it or not. You were with us during the writing of this book as a coach with The Author Incubator. You and Megan Jo Wilson were with me through Miracle Minded Coaching. To all my fellow cohorts in the coaching course and the writing course. Your support and friendships have been invaluable during this process.

To The Gestalt International Study Center for getting me off to a great start in coaching. For providing me with a solid foundation and template to help people find happiness and awareness in their life through coaching, using the Gestalt Core Concepts and Behaviors.

To all the coaching clients who allowed us to use their stories in this book to let readers know they are not alone in their journey to awareness. Help and guidance is there for the asking.

A special thanks to Mary Anne Walk, my mentor, coach, and dear friend. You have supported me with your kindness, experience, and trust since we met. You can't make this stuff up!

To Ivan, Dagny, Phil, and Sandra, who were there from the beginning of this journey.

To my inner circle of friends on this topic, Steeve, Tom, Kelly, Butch, Kathy, Steve, Lynn, Claire, Brian, Julie, Mike, Karen, Tazeen, Jayne, Elizabeth, Lise, Victoria, Tiara, Vicky, and many more. We are all doing the best we can with the awareness we have.

To my partner, Liz, who loves unconditionally. She was a sixth-grade teacher for thirty-eight years. She is now retired and is my teacher in life. She holds the house and home together like no one I have ever seen. She loves me like I've never been loved before. She lets me be myself and as you have read my stories, that is not an easy task.

# ABOUT THE AUTHORS

## SPENCER BARTON

Spencer Alden Barton is from Yarmouth, Maine. He graduated from high school at North Yarmouth Academy and is, at time of writing, on leave from Worcester Polytechnic Institute. He has spent this time renovating his workshop, working for a local building contractor, learning more about ADHD, and, of course, researching and writing for The

Father, The Son, and the Aha Moment. Spencer loves building things and helping people, and he hopes this book will help many people to find the aha moments that he and his father have shared.

## STEVE BARTON

Steve Spencer Barton is a native to Maine. He is a resident of Westbrook. Steve was born on Labor Day, September 2, 1956.

After receiving his BA in business management from The University of Southern Maine, Steve went into the family flower business, Barton's Flowers of Westbrook. In 1979, When Steve was twenty-three, his father had a major stroke and Steve accepted the position to manage the family business.

In 1985, he and his father purchased Harmon's Flowers of Portland. Merging the two companies to what is now Harmon Floral Company. In November 2007, he and his father sold the company.

With an enduring love of business and a strong desire to help people personally and professionally, he began coaching individuals and business owners based on his backgrounds in mindset and company management. Steve is a passionate seeker of truth regarding human behavior and psychology. He is particularly experienced in helping individuals and teams to connect with their innate awareness. He calls this a commonsense approach to what is not all that common.

In May 2015, Steve graduated the eight-month intensive coaching program from the Gestalt International Study Center in Wellfleet, Massachusetts, giving him a foundation in the Gestalt model and the Gestalt Core Concepts and Behaviors to work from.

In September 2021, Steve graduated from Miracle Minded Coaching with Marianne Williamson and the team at Difference Press, giving him an even wider range of coaching skills to use with his clients.

Currently, Steve is the owner of Steve Barton Coaching, which provides coaching for individuals, businesses, and groups.

Steve has registered with the United States Trademark Office, a process that he uses in his coaching practice. It is in the format of a psychological game and mindset practice. It is called The Game of Ten®. His hope is to train others to teach this process to the psychological, coaching, and wellness community. His website is www.OverTheLookingGlass.com.

# ABOUT DIFFERENCE PRESS

Difference Press is the exclusive publishing arm of The Author Incubator, an educational company for entrepreneurs – including life coaches, healers, consultants, and community leaders – looking for a comprehensive solution to get their books written, published, and promoted. Its founder, Dr. Angela Lauria, has been bringing to life the literary ventures of hundreds of authors-in-transformation since 1994.

A boutique-style self-publishing service for clients of The Author Incubator, Difference Press boasts a fair and easy-to-understand profit structure, low-priced author copies, and author-friendly contract terms. Most importantly, all of our #incubatedauthors maintain ownership of their copyright at all times.

## LET'S START A MOVEMENT WITH YOUR MESSAGE

In a market where hundreds of thousands of books are published every year and are never heard from again, The Author Incubator is different. Not only do all Difference

Press books reach Amazon bestseller status, but all of our authors are actively changing lives and making a difference.

Since launching in 2013, we've served over 500 authors who came to us with an idea for a book and were able to write it and get it self-published in less than six months. In addition, more than 100 of those books were picked up by traditional publishers and are now available in bookstores. We do this by selecting the highest quality and highest potential applicants for our future programs.

Our program doesn't only teach you how to write a book – our team of coaches, developmental editors, copy editors, art directors, and marketing experts incubate you from having a book idea to being a published, best-selling author, ensuring that the book you create can actually make a difference in the world. Then we give you the training you need to use your book to make the difference in the world, or to create a business out of serving your readers.

## ARE YOU READY TO MAKE A DIFFERENCE?

You've seen other people make a difference with a book. Now it's your turn. If you are ready to stop watching and start taking massive action, go to http://theauthorincubator.com/apply/.

"Yes, I'm ready."

## OTHER BOOKS BY DIFFERENCE PRESS

*The Scholarship Playbook for Parents of Student-Athletes: Stop Fouling Out and Start Scoring Money for College* by Dr. Simoné Edwards

*When Marriage Needs a Miracle: The Modern Woman's Guide to Figure out the Future of Your Relationship* by Shari Kubinec

*Conquer the Classroom: How to Manage Your Students, Your Administration, and Yourself* by Robin Reed Riggle, B.F.A., M.Ed.

# THANK YOU

We want to thank you so much for reading *The Father, the Son, and the Aha Moment: Tools for Helping You and Your Child Develop a Path to Happiness*. If you've made it this far, we know one of two things about you. First, you're more ready than ever to experience parenting your child in a different way. And second, maybe you also start at the end of the book before diving in. (Hey, me too!)

We would love to learn more about your journeys and successes in pursuing your dreams. Please keep in touch (I'm most active on Facebook and Instagram and LinkedIn), share your wins, and visit www.TheGameOfTen.com for more resources, including a Discovery Form to see where you are in The Game of Ten.

You may also go to the website to book a free half-hour session to talk and see if it makes sense for us to work together.

Made in the USA
Monee, IL
10 February 2022